M000009216

God's Favorite Prayers

Tzvee Zahavy

Talmudic Books

GOD'S FAVORITE PRAYERS © 2011 by Tzvee Zahavy. All rights reserved. Printed in the United States of America. No part of this book may be used or reproduced in any manner whatsoever without written permission except in the case of brief quotations embodied in critical articles and reviews. For information, address Talmudic Books Inc., 1391 Milford Terrace. Teaneck, NJ 07666. Internet: www.talmudicbooks.com.

Talmudic books may be purchased for educational, business, or sales promotional use. For information, please write Special Markets Department, Talmudic Books Inc., 1391 Milford Terrace, Teaneck, NJ 07666.

FIRST EDITION
ISBN: 978-0-615-50949-5

Contents

INVITATION... 1

BEGINNING 7

THE PRAYER BOOK... 17

THE PERFORMER'S PRAYERS 25

THE MYSTIC'S PRAYERS 53

THE SCRIBE'S PRAYERS 71

THE PRIEST'S PRAYERS 89

THE MEDITATOR'S PRAYERS 111

THE CELEBRITY'S PRAYERS 127

THE KIDDUSH 145

THE SHOFAR... 153

SOURCES.. 155

ABOUT THE AUTHOR.. 156

REVIEWS.. 157

For all the people
who faithfully engage
in serving the community

Invitation

I invite you into the heart of Jewish spirituality, to learn about its idiom and imagery, its emotions and its great sweeping dramas. I invite you to meet six ideal personalities of Jewish prayer. And I invite you to get to know some of their respective prayers.

My thesis in this book is simple. Jews pray every day in holy synagogues and in ordinary places throughout the world. When they do so, they engage in sacred rituals and they recite and sing and meditate prayers that derive from six distinct archetypes. I invite you to meet the six personalities: the performer, the mystic, the scribe, the priest, the meditator and the celebrity.

My approach in this book is also simple. I use stories, anecdotes and personal references throughout this volume. But this work is not a personal memoir. My narrative framework in the text will help guide you to discover some deep and personal meanings in the classic Jewish liturgies.

I will tell you about a few of my experiences and several of my outstanding teachers to motivate your interest and humanize what can be difficult and abstract prayers. In the past, a lot of dry theological approaches have been applied to the readings of the liturgy. As a result, in our synagogues, it is common to hear that many are bored with the services or alienated from them.

My point is that liturgy is not dry theology. It is a vibrant enterprise of bright ways of expression, filled with colorful pictures, evoking sentiments and passions and full of exhilaration. To appreciate great prayers, people need to stop, to find their own personal threads of liturgical meanings and to discover all of its energy and excitement.

I invite lay people, educators and academics, Jews and non-Jews to come with me and start this process through my set here of contemporary metaphors and anecdotal narratives which I wrap around my presentations and analyses of the main prayers of Jewish worship.

I invite you to join me in these main steps of my investigations in this book, my quest to discover the beauty and meaning of God's favorite prayers.

In my opening chapter, I tell you a bit about who I am, with short stories of aspects of my childhood and younger years when I sought spiritual textures and began my search for the perfect *shul*, the Yiddish word for synagogue. That is when I started exploring both the actual and ideal social networks of the synagogue.

I invite you to join with me as I recall parts of the dramatic arc of my expeditions of discovery that I unfold for you in this book. When I was younger, I mistakenly thought I could find a perfect brick and mortar synagogue. Inevitably that led me both to discovery and to disappointment, followed by growth and a realization that I need to conduct another kind of search.

To open the way for new thinking about the old formalized prayers, I start out to address the prayer book in the chapter that follows and to explain why I find the regular, more common ways of talking about prayer lacking, which is why I do not follow some of the paths of previous explorers and travelers.

In my discussion about the recent prayer book edition of the Chief Rabbi of the British Empire, I clarify why theologians don't always speak straightforwardly about the liturgy. I then discuss how at times the sermons of rabbis in synagogues are diversions away from the spirituality of prayer.

Next I defend my view that reconstructing the history of liturgy is mostly beyond our reach. I speak about prayer as timeless and without visible origins. Finally, in my consideration of one recent popular way to classify prayers, I make clear why that particular previous try to formulate categories for sorting out the liturgy doesn't edify us that much. All of this initial groundwork shows you why we need a new paradigm of interpretation for the prayer book and for what goes on in the synagogue.

In the next six chapters, I present accounts of my avid spiritual quests for God's favorite prayers and for an ideal synagogue. These sections of the book unfold for you in my six encounters with exemplary places, people and prayers. That allows me to convey to you what I learned about *the six archetypes of Jewish prayer*. I call them the six people you meet in synagogue.

In my reports on these people who pray and their prayers, I introduce you to the most important spiritual individuals that I have come to know. You will meet exemplary real people and their respective ideal types and their prayers, the essential components of Jewish spirituality. Here are their appellations and a capsule itinerary of our spiritual quest.

In the introduction to my first account, I introduce a wonderful cantor, Louis Danto, whom I heard when I was young in the Atlantic Beach Jewish Center on Long Island in New York State. I tell you about that summer congregation where I spent the years of my childhood. I invite you there to encounter the archetypal worshipper that I name 'the performer.' In that report, we then learn about the central roles that the Tanakh, the Hebrew Bible, plays in the synagogue. In that context I speak about the Torah readings in the synagogue, the bar and bat mitzvah, and some of the prayers of Rosh Hashanah, namely the Musaf (Additional Service) which accompanies the blowing of the *shofar,* the ram's horn.

In the opening of my second account, I introduce Hannah, both as a biblical figure and as my theoretical model of a type of prayer. I discuss the story of Hannah in the Biblical narrative in the book of Samuel. Then I encounter a contemporary Hannah in a small *shul* in Jerusalem called Har-El. This is where I invite you to meet the archetype of Jewish prayer that I term 'the mystic.' In that context, I speak about the Kaddish prayer and other mystical parts of the liturgies. I explain there also, using other examples of Jewish prayers, how the mythic mode of the religious imagination operates in the synagogue.

In the introduction to my third account, I recall one of my beloved teachers, Rabbi Aharon Lichtenstein. I talk about meeting him in another *shul* in Jerusalem, a few blocks from Har-El, known as the Shtiblach in Old Katamon. There we encounter together another ideal Jew at prayer; this one, I entitle 'the scribe.' I examine the personality of that archetype, his values and theologies. I discuss the Shema prayer, that core confession of the Jewish faith, and other scribal elements in the prayer book and in the Passover Seder.

In my fourth report, I introduce a generic priest whom I call Mr. Cohen (*cohen* in Hebrew is the word for priest). We meet him in an abstract synagogue. This opens up my discussion of the ideal Jewish type that I call 'the priest.' I examine the identifiable personality of that archetype, his agenda of values and his overt theologies. I explain the genetics of actual priestly descent and the historical roots of this personality in ancient Israel. In that context, I discuss the Amidah prayer, a solemn centerpiece recitation of each synagogue service.

Then I go on to introduce what I call the avatars of the priest. These are other embodiments and personifications of the archetype in the synagogue liturgy and in ancient, rabbinic and modern contexts. I range through Jewish history and draw illustrations from the dramatic biblical story of Esther to the victory of the Maccabees, from the disputes of the rabbis of the Talmud to the resistance of some Jews to the Nazis in the Holocaust. I conclude that report with a recollection of my father's formal *shul* in New York City, Congregation Zichron Ephraim. I recall how he officiated there elegantly in the mode of the priestly archetype.

In the introduction to my fifth report, I present the archetype that I identify as 'the meditator' and call Deborah. I use this as an occasion to develop my innovative notions that rabbinic blessings themselves serve as the meditative components of Jewish living both outside and inside the synagogue.

I expand on how blessings serve as constant triggers of mindful meditation. I scrutinize how blessings in general— and the grace after eating in particular—function as exemplary vehicles for meditation and for fostering compassion in Judaic worship. In an imagined debate, I contrast this practice with a form of mindful meditation that is drawn from a Buddhist context.

In the opening to my sixth report, I describe some ad hoc non-synagogue prayer services, a *davening* that took place on a Tower Air charter jet flight to Israel. There, in 1982, I prayed the morning liturgy in a makeshift *minyan* at the back of the plane with nine other Jews. I introduce you to one of the real participants in that *davening*, Rabbi Meir Kahane. He was a radical Jewish activist and politician who years later was tragically murdered. I take you up there on the plane ride also to meet the ideal type that I label 'the celebrity-monotheist.' In that context, I discuss the Aleinu, the exit-prayer of every synagogue gathering, and I summarize the triumphal and messianic values of this ideal type. I extend this discussion to consider how some prayers treat the subject of martyrdom within the synagogue services.

At the conclusion of our quest, I gather our six archetype-friends after synagogue services for an imaginary debate of their perspectives on redemption, the messiah and the Messianic Age. Then, to show an example of how the diverse archetypes of the synagogue come together in the drama of the real liturgy, I end with a presentation of the prayers that accompany the *shofar* blowing at the conclusion of Yom Kippur.

I use those real and imagined places of worship, those real and hypothetical people, and those very real Jewish prayers to create recognizable and distinct settings. This allows me to recreate and depict for you the six most vivid variations on the sacred modalities that I discovered in my voyages into Jewish worship and spirituality—the performer, mystic, scribe, priest, meditator and celebrity—the primary friends in the social network of the synagogue and their respective prayers.

If you are a praying Jew, the texts I consider will be familiar to you. If you are new to the Siddur, be assured that I shall present the selections from the liturgies to you as I go forward, along with my explanations, insights and suggestions.

Over years of devotion and contemplation, I have discovered within myself and in my communities of prayer these archetypes of the Siddur and of the synagogue. Through this process of discovery, my religious consciousness has expanded, and ever so slightly I have come closer to God and found value in some of his favorite prayers.

I invite you to come along now as I narrate the high points of my studies and journeys, explaining more about what I mean by "archetypes" and how, one-by-one, you can become acquainted with them, agree with them, argue with them, learn from them and, perhaps, pray with them.

Beginning

da·ven ['dɑvən]

intr.v. **da·vened**, **da·ven·ing**, **da·vens**
1. To recite Jewish liturgical prayers.
2. To sway or rock lightly.
 [From the Yiddish davnen, דאַוונען.]
Da'ven·er *n.*

syn·a·gogue
1. A building or place of meeting for worship and religious instruction in the Jewish faith.
2. A congregation of Jews for the purpose of worship or religious study.
3. The Jewish religion as organized or typified in local congregations.

—The American Heritage Dictionary of the English Language, 2009

I was born Jewish and raised in an Orthodox Jewish family, but not an entirely stereotypical one. My mother grew up as an American-born Reform Jew in Washington Heights in Upper Manhattan. She went to New York City public schools and then got her BA and MA degrees at Hunter College. My father was reared in an American-Orthodox family. Both of his parents were born in the U.S. He too went to New York City public schools, then to a yeshiva for high school and to Yeshiva University for his college degree, for his rabbinic ordination and for his PhD.

At some point, my young professional mother enrolled in a Hebrew class that my young rabbi dad was teaching. Romance followed. After they married, my mom became Orthodox in her faith and practice. In her role as a dutiful rabbi's wife, she obtained the venerable honorary title of *rebbetzin*.

For an American Jewish family like my dad's to retain its orthodoxy was not a common story during the decades of the great assimilation prior to WWII. The currents sweeping Jews away from religion were strong during that era. But my mom and dad swam against the currents. I inherited a strong commitment to Judaism from both of my parents.

I was born on the Upper West Side of Manhattan, where my father was a dynamic figure on the New York rabbinical scene. He served as a rabbi for two decades, from 1941 to 1961. First, before he married, he played rabbi out in the "minor leagues" in small Jewish communities in Lexington, Kentucky and Omaha, Nebraska. After that, he served in the "big leagues" in pulpits in Orthodox synagogues in New York City. He presided first on New York's West Side at the West Side Institutional Synagogue (WSIS) as assistant rabbi.

It was there in 1947 that he changed his name from Goldstein to Zahavy. He was inspired by the Zionist movement and felt the calling to Hebraize his name, as many other activists and visionaries of that era did.

The senior rabbi at the WSIS was the well-known Rabbi Herbert S. Goldstein. When my dad started to serve as a rabbi there, he approached Rabbi Goldstein and told him of his motivations and his idealistic plans to change his name to Zahavy.

The senior Rabbi Goldstein endorsed my father's idealism and then suggested another more mundane motivation for his support of the planned name change. Partly in jest, he explained to the junior rabbi that he had been concerned. If a check had come in to the synagogue made out to Rabbi Goldstein, he had feared that, with two rabbis of the same name, there might be some confusion. Hence, he was happy to hear that my father was going to change his name.

After his stint at the WSIS, my rising-star dad moved uptown a few blocks to Congregation Ohev Zedek, where he was appointed associate rabbi. Following that, he moved on to assume the pulpit as senior rabbi at the swanky Upper East Side Congregation Zichron Ephraim (now named the Park East Synagogue).

From the age of three, I grew up on the East Side on Sixty-eighth Street and Third Avenue, in New York's so-called silk stocking congressional district. Not a very spiritual setting. There were few Orthodox children around for me to play with in my neighborhood. Many of Manhattan's Orthodox families lived down on the Lower East Side or uptown on the West Side. I attended Manhattan Day School, a progressive Zionist oriented elementary yeshiva day school on the west side of the park.

Spiritual Textures

Even with my varied background, like most Orthodox Jews I spent a whole lot of time in synagogues when I was growing up. As a son of a rabbi, I'm sure that I sat for more time in a house of worship than the average Jewish kid. As a child, my mother schlepped me to *shul* every *Shabbos* (the Yiddish word for Sabbath), and I sat mostly quietly and listened to the cantors chant the formal services, leading the members in prayer. I followed along as the expert readers chanted from the Torah scroll. I heard as the *shammoses* (i.e., ritual directors, also called sextons or beadles) recited the *Kaddishes*, as they led the mourners in their obligatory recitations of a prayer for their deceased loved ones.

I was mainly a well-behaved kid who sat attentively through the weekly Sabbath Torah readings and the *haftorah, the* chantings from the Prophets. I heard the Rosh Hashanah *shofar* blowings, taking all of this quite seriously, in accord with what I was taught at home and in school. I marched in the Simchat Torah *Hakafot,* those parades when the adult worshippers joyously carried the scrolls as they marched and danced around the synagogue. We children were allowed to carry and wave paper Israeli, American and holiday Simchat Torah flags that were pasted to thin wooden sticks. As we pranced around the synagogue with our flags, sometimes we fenced with them and looked for trouble.

During the summers, we went to our Long Island summer home in Atlantic Beach. The sleepy Jewish community in that village boasted a single centrally located and nicely maintained rectangular brick synagogue. By design, it was kept Orthodox in its ritual and services so that one inclusive house of worship could serve the whole community, from the more liberal Reform and Conservative to its few ardently religious Jews. Men and women sat separately. But, unlike in other Orthodox *shuls*, there was no physical wall divider between the sexes. Most of the villagers in fact were not Orthodox in their practices. They'd go home after prayers on Saturday morning and head off quite openly to the beach or to golf, tennis, biking on the boardwalk, shopping or other ordinary weekend activities not normally practiced by Orthodox Jews on the Sabbath.

During those summers out in Atlantic Beach, we happily attended the weekly Sabbath services at the Jewish Center. Back then, it was a well-to-do community, without too much ostentation. To attract worshippers, the *shul* offered a Kiddush collation after the Saturday morning services, and I made sure to fill up a wax paper cup with sarsaparilla soda to go along with my little rectangle of sponge cake and my handful of salty, dry, octagonal Manischewitz Tam Tam crackers. I never touched the creamed herring and did not care much for the little gefilte fish balls that they put out on platters to the delight of the hungry congregants after their lengthy prayers.

While I sat in these sundry synagogues as a child, yes, I became familiar with the services and fluent in the liturgy. That turned out later to be both an advantage and a disadvantage to my spiritual growth. Indeed, I could participate, perform and lead the synagogue worship in Hebrew. I knew the tunes, the words, and the cadences. But as I grew older and wanted to find more substance, I learned that adult meaning does not flow easily out of what you learn as a child. Later on, it turned out to be quite complex and daunting to open the book of devotion that I knew nearly by heart, that represented what the Jewish tradition calls the "worship of the heart" and try to turn my mind on it, to study it in a mature manner. And I found that it was harder yet for me to extract an adult's spiritual experience from the services of these synagogues that I had gotten to know when I was a kid.

Perfect Prayer

Fast forward now to a particularly intense stage of my spiritual life, in 1978. I was on a leave for six months from my teaching and went to live in Jerusalem with my wife and two young children. I decided on an ambitious program—to try to pray at least one time in every one of the synagogues in Jerusalem, the most sacred city in Judaism.

That capital city of Judaism has dozens of varieties of *shuls* for all kinds of worship styles of the various and sundry communities who live there, side-by-side, mostly with mutual respect and in harmony with one another.

During that phase of my life, I imagined in an especially colorful way that I was engaged in a big international quest for a perfect religious experience. In a particularly fanciful fashion, I saw my professed search as a parallel to the one Bruce Brown catalogued in the great film *Endless Summer*. This famous 1966 documentary film follows two surfers, Michael Hynson and Robert August, on a quest to find the perfect wave. The film documented the two boys searching the globe for simple perfection in their quasi-mystical sport. The movie site IMDB sums up the story of the film, "Brown follows two young surfers around the world in search of the perfect wave, and ends up finding quite a few, in addition to some colorful local characters."

Back then, the film spoke to those of us who were young seekers, as it did for many others of that idealistic age. Of course, the core of the sport of surfing is the wave and, no doubt, the lover of surfing wants to embark on the quest for the best possible wave. To find and surf the perfect wave is to experience the performance of the quintessence of the sport. I adored that classic Bruce Brown film, with its humor and charm that thinly cloaked a more serious story of sportsmen seeking a form of ultimate perfection in their beloved pastime.

My involvement with surfing was not just as a filmgoer or mere observer. I actually had taken up the sport of surfing in Atlantic Beach when I was a teenager. One summer, I bought my friend's used surfboard for twenty dollars. I dutifully waxed its surface so I could stand on it without slipping and take it out in the ocean in the evening. I'd then visualize as if I was a California or Hawaii surfer dude out in the big surf. Actually, I was waiting for the little two-foot local Long Island South Shore waves to sweep me lazily back to shore. That was fun, and a way to pass the summer times. But, even with my healthy and vivid imagination at work, all that activity did not become for me a quest of any sort for realization of a surfing goal.

Yet, later on, the experience served me well. My paltry surfing life, along with the basic narrative of *The Endless Summer,* helped me to form a valid metaphor for what I was seeking in my travels, searching for the perfect spiritual wave—the ideal *davening* (that great Yiddish word for Jewish prayer) at the ultimate synagogue.

As I saw it, a few years after my teen years in Atlantic Beach, I did embark on a quest in search of that different sort of perfect wave. I spent months and years of travel and research sabbaticals seeking, among other things in life, the perfect wave in a *shul,* the swaying and the praying that hit the mark, that stayed in the groove, and that fulfilled the quest of the endless *davener.*

And, like the surfers in the film who found their perfect wave at an out-of-the-way beach at Cape St. Francis in South Africa, during a chapter of my own quest, I once found a single, perfect mystical place of worship at a small, off-the-beaten-path synagogue in Jerusalem.

I did get to quite a few synagogues in Jerusalem that year. There were big and formal ones, small and simple ones, Ashkenazic ones (representing the European style of prayer), Sephardic ones (after the Oriental style), Hasidic in the nineteenth-century Polish fashion of those ultra-Orthodox Jews, and Yemenite in the style of the Jews of some Arab lands. Of course, there were standardized services of prayer outdoors at the Western Wall of Temple in the Old City of Jerusalem, there were regular services in some school auditoriums and there were a few American style Reform and Conservative congregations. I got to pray at many of these and found them often welcoming and satisfying, charming, relaxing, comfortable and, occasionally, frustrating, opaque and foreign.

Wouldn't you know it, the best of all those choices for me, at that time and place, was a congregation in my own backyard. I found something special at a compact little synagogue called Har-El, around the corner from my apartment on Hapalmach Street in Jerusalem. This was a simple one-room *shul*-house structure. Its exterior was Jerusalem stone like most of the buildings in the area. That kind of pale limestone had been used in buildings in the city from ancient times. Inside, the little synagogue had a one-wire electric heater affixed to the wall at the front of the room and no fancy fixtures or trimmings anywhere to be found. The pews were simple fold-down hardwood seats. Each place to sit had a cubby in front of it, hanging from the back of the next pew forward. On top of that cubby was a wood stand on which you could rest your prayer book. A plain eternal lamp, with a flickering bulb to simulate a candle, hung above a basic light hued wooden ark that housed the Torah at the front of the sanctuary.

The women sat in the back, behind the several rows that made up the men's section of the *shul*. The gender divider of the synagogue, the *mechitzah*, was a solid wood partition along the bottom with a translucent cloth curtain on the top half, allowing the few rows of women a veiled line of sight and audibility to the men's prayers up front.

Let me be prompt to add that, even though I'm not at all happy with the segregation of the sexes in the Orthodox synagogue, I won't digress to delve into that issue in this book. I'm hoping that the insights I share in this work are equally accessible and meaningful to all who wish to find them, regardless of gender, age, denomination, religion, or any other differentiating factor.

At Har-El, the few windows along the sides of the room were made of frosted jalousie glass slats that we opened and closed by rotating their small handles. In the center of the *shul*, the *bimah* platform for reading the Torah and reciting the prayers was modest in size and undecorated. All-in-all, the place had a kind of Amish or Puritan simplicity to it.

Most of the members of that *minyan* were established Israeli Orthodox Jews whose parents or grandparents originally derived from Western European roots. With few exceptions, these worshippers were not recent Anglo or French immigrants, not Sephardic, and not Hasidic. The parishioners knew each other from the neighborhood and respected each other with a formal civility that one had to witness to appreciate.

Back then, it hit me that this was the right mix of the perfect *minyan* for me. These were my analogs to Bruce Brown's gang of surfers and to the "colorful local characters" that they met. They were people of different histories and stories but all with shared religious propensities, skills and needs. In this brief snapshot of time and place, clerks and professors, accountants and bankers, business owners, contractors, rabbis and craftsmen joined as one every day in their counterpart activity to surfing—to recite and sing their familiar prayers.

This flock of like-minded peers prayed in the same way, with just the right measure of fervor and with staunch confidence in their mastery of the ins and outs of the liturgy. These people showed no overt interest in petty or grand political divisions or quarrels. They were sincere believers and pure practitioners of Orthodox Judaism in their slice of the universe.

Day after day, I'd go to this little *shul* to pray, and it never varied. I was on no account ever disappointed. I imagined in retrospect that it was as if I had found a beach where I went out into the surf and, every day, the waves were perfect.

That one season of mystical satisfaction for this "Endless *Davener*" (that Yiddish word for a person praying) proved to me that, yes, the perfect prayer does exist; it was serene and smooth and seamless. The equilibrium and numinous quality of Har-El was still there for me for a while; and then, alas, when I returned and visited a few years later in 1986, it was gone.

No, the *shul* building was still there (and is there now) and many of the same characters were still *davening* there. But other congregants had joined the mix and a few improvements had been made to the small sanctuary. A serious heating unit had been installed and, as it turned out for me, worst of all, they put into the wall a spell-breaking air conditioning unit.

Soon after my arrival back in Jerusalem in the hot summer of 1986, I went to Har-El to pray. I wanted so much to ride again the perfect wave of *davening* that I knew from the past. The service started out as I remembered, and all the spiritual and mystical feelings started welling up within me. And then I watched as one, two and three people politely got up during our first few minutes of prayers to adjust the plastic A/C cooling ducts. First, a familiar looking person whom I knew from the bank got up to point the ducts in his chosen direction, and then another synagogue member who lived in my building arose and moved them to blow the air in another route. It unnerved me as I imagined surfers who did not like the way the waves were breaking on that legendary beach in South Africa, paddled out and tried to move some rocks in the jetty to redirect the curl of the perfect wave. No, I wanted to tell them, you were not there to tamper with the natural way that the wave formed and moved towards the shore.

One after another after another, the same simple surfers in the *shul* tried to make over the context of the perfect wave to their preferences. On account of the tinkering with an insignificant air flow, I saw the unity that I imagined in the congregation dissipate. A new technology had disrupted my spirituality. It went poof—and the magic spell was broken, the tides had shifted, and the well formed wave that once was, could not be recovered again. As if surfers had tried to fiddle with the settings of their waves, I felt that the members at Har-El had lost track of some of the small essences of their endeavors, the act of their surfing the waves of spirituality, the core of their *davening*. Yes, of course, all of this was in my head, my subjective judgment and not some special insight into anyone else's spiritual being. Yet for me, it looked like my ephemeral quest for an exceptional spiritual pursuit had to move on then to another venue.

I did continue my journey around Jerusalem—and the world—in search of perfect religious waves, and I did find a few more good ones. In the process, I got to meet some colorful real people and, on top of that, from all my searching, I derived another benefit. From what I saw and felt during all of that travel, I started to formulate more clearly my understandings of ideals, of the archetypal surfers in the synagogue.

We leave Jerusalem on this note that the spiritual contents of religious experience, like all of the subjective experiences of life, indeed can be passing and short-lived.

Later in our narrative, I will come back with you to Har-El and talk more in depth about my meeting with the ideal type I call the mystic, and to explore with you further the dimensions of that singular character of Jewish spirituality.

During my quest, I uncovered new dimensions in my own faith; I found out that my religion in its essence is not composed only of abstract philosophy or solely out of a set of religious rules. I've obtained that Judaism is better understood to me as the *collective* thoughts and activity of a group of diverse people and personalities, like the six memorable ones that I met along the way. I introduce them to you soon, one-by-one, along with their prayers and mannerisms. I tell you how I met them, how I got to know them and, through them, how I learned about my own relationship with God.

But as we prepare to set out on our quest, I need first to tell you about the prayer book and, in that context, about some familiar paths into the discussion of Jewish prayer that we will *not* explore because I have found them to be spiritual blind alleys.

The Prayer Book

Siddur

A prayer book containing prayers for the various days of the year.

—The American Heritage Dictionary

The Chief Rabbi of the British Empire, Sir Jonathan Sacks, begins his introduction to the *Koren Sacks Siddur* (Jerusalem, 2009) entitled, "Understanding Jewish Prayer," with the poetic statement that "Prayer is the language of the soul in conversation with God. It is the most intimate gesture of the religious life, and the most transformative." The introduction goes on in lofty terms and continues for a page or two with additional prosaic statements such as, "Language is the bridge joining us to Infinity."

When the rabbi turns to speak about the Siddur itself, the Jewish prayer book, he says to start with, "The Siddur is the choral symphony the covenantal people has sung to God across forty centuries from the days of the patriarchs until the present day." He calls it a "calibrated harmony."

To be sure, this essay is the sage rabbi's lyrical introduction to the prayer services of the Jews. It is a flowery prologue, meant to be consumed by the faithful. I don't want to parse its every expressive phrase, can one ever disagree with poetry? I must say though that I don't think the Siddur is a magnificent symphony festooned with harmonies. I'm certain the rabbi is on the right track, but he stops off at the wrong metaphor.

The Siddur is neither a "symphony" nor a "harmony"; as I see it, the Siddur's prayer service zigs when it should zag. It starts and stops and restarts. It changes the topic of conversation and presentation abruptly and frequently. It meanders and wanders across expanses of time and space. It contradicts and repeats in patterns that seem to have no peers.

Later in his essay, Rabbi Sacks appears to recognize this as he surprisingly discusses the relationship between prayer and the iterative mathematical patterns known as fractals. A fractal is a rough or fragmented geometric shape that can be looked at more closely in every one of its parts. Each small element of a fractal is approximately a smaller copy of the whole.

As he draws on a high level from concepts associated with mathematical chaos theory, the rabbi seems to be saying that, in an inexact way, the fractal serves as an approximate metaphoric portrayal of the landscape of the Siddur. But he abruptly stops this discourse on the comparison of prayer to fractal after a few short paragraphs, without much explanation, leaving off from his provocative metaphoric suggestions. The Chief Rabbi draws back into a more comfortable position and says again that he sees in the Jewish prayer book a masterpiece of magnificence with a single rising crescendo of intensity and expression.

I struggle sincerely with this portrayal. I do want to afford the learned rabbi the respect and authority that his office merits. But, at last, I have to say, "Step back please. Open the book and look again at the words." You don't need to be a rocket scientist or a Chief Rabbi to see what lies before you. On the one hand, the metaphor that describes it does not need to be as complex as a fractal image. On the other hand, the prayer services should not be likened to a single musical work. The Jewish prayer book must be compared to something a bit more complex than a unitary musical composition.

Let me start over and describe the Siddur in metaphors as I see them. This collection of prayers is more than a raucous script. We use this composite book of texts in our synagogues as an inharmonious set of consecutive performances.

Imagine that you walked into a synagogue—unfamiliar with the rites—and further imagine that you did not understand a word of Hebrew. What would you see and hear? In jarring sequences, you would see Jews stand and sit, and then stand again. You would see them fall on their faces, acting out dejection. They would open cabinet doors and close doors, march around, carry and touch objects, read from a scroll, kiss the fringes of their garments and cover their eyes and, throughout all that, they would chant, sing, be silent, and chant again.

You would see them start to pray in the morning service on page one and then, eighty-eight pages later, you would hear the leader call out, "Bless!" meaning, let us now start to pray! Those previous words, it turns out, were just preliminary. During all of this action and recitation, those Jews who were reciting the prayers would move around, shake and shiver, rock and roll.

In respectful disagreement with the Chief Rabbi, I would rather characterize what goes on in the public presentation of the Jewish prayer services more colorfully as follows:

Come to the synagogue to witness a rock festival with six bands performing. Each presentation has its own sound, lyrics and style. I will show you in the coming chapters that, in the Siddur and the synagogue, I see a book and its performances that make up a complex set of multiple voices. Sometimes, the personalities behind those voices speak to one another or perform together. Oftentimes, they sing past one another, separately and apart.

The services in the synagogue that I know comprise a sort of Woodstock Festival of Jews at prayer, not a seamless symphony and not a choppy cacophony, as synagogue prayer is a concert venue with multiple performances. Looked at as a whole, I see it as a series of events accompanied by some dissonance and disharmony. Yet I am sure each of its parts has its own musical coherence and a synchronization that I need to discover and appreciate.

By design, Rabbi Sacks got his metaphors wide of the mark. He is not alone to be faulted. When all is said and done, he is the chief of the promoters of the good aspects and aesthetics of the Jewish faith. Many other theologians with the same intent have previously sought to describe the services of the Siddur as a linear symphony, to impose upon them a synchronicity that really is not there. I do understand that the rabbis would like the performances of the synagogue to be magnificent and artistically nonpareil. Okay, I want the same.

Perhaps the Chief Rabbi never went to an inspired music event with multiple bands in performance. The tunes the groups play in turn at such a venue absolutely do not mesh like a symphony. The artists, in their distinctive groups, positively do not fit together. But the artistic and emotional impact of the components of such an occasion— independently, and as one entity—often can pack quite a wallop. And for the attendee-participant it can be both stunning and inspirational.

In a composite rock or pop or jazz experience, it does not detract that the vehicles themselves speak in many voices and sing in dozens of dissonant keys. In our synagogue services too, the whirling activity of reading and singing and humming and silence, we can find and mine a trove of truly complex and fascinating contents of words, ideas, themes, tropes and compositions—each one an inspiring act unto itself.

Like a great impresario's rock happening, the great Jewish get-together called the synagogue hosts performances that convey a multiplicity of ideas, precepts and personalities. That's a big part of what I describe in this book.

One thing I will not dwell on in my account is the role of the rabbi in all the excitement of Jewish prayer in the synagogue. Let me justify why I leave out the rabbi from the primary list of people that I meet in the synagogue. Though now people routinely associate a rabbi with his or her synagogue, throughout history the pulpit rabbi was *not* integral to the Jewish prayer that was performed in that place of worship. The rabbi today may routinely preach to his congregation during the service. Indeed, there is evidence that people gave sermons in synagogues two millennia in the past; the Talmud mentions that expositions on biblical topics were delivered in synagogues and the New Testament describes Jesus and Paul preaching to Jews in synagogues in Israel and Asia Minor.

The practice of regular sermonizing looks as if it changed over history. Ismar Elbogen, the great historian of Jewish liturgy, says that "The manner of the sermon changed in the course of time with changing tastes; in some districts it was nearly completely neglected for centuries" (*Jewish Liturgy*, Phila., 1993, p. 157).

The modern rabbi's sermon was reintroduced in the past century, beginning with its reemergence in Reform Temples, some assume, to keep up with the same type of practice in

Protestant and Catholic churches. It is accurate to say then that the rabbi's sermon is an "optional" element in the synagogue service. In fact, it is not referred to as a scheduled event in any Siddur that I know of.

I've observed that, when the modern rabbi gets up to speak in synagogue, he or she may in fact distract the congregants from the standard performances of prayer. I'd hazard a guess that, back in the first century, when Jesus and Paul delivered their sermons in synagogues, more than a few Jews of that time thought those teachers were seeking to divert them from the traditional ways of worship.

In truth, sermons are not *davening*; they are not liturgy. Accordingly, I am not accustomed to meeting a preaching rabbi as a distinct archetype of prayer in my synagogue. Now, after saying that, I must add that, in my discussions below, I will refer to a few prominent rabbis who, in their praying, take on the personae of the core archetypes that we meet. I will speak about my father and two of my teachers to illustrate three of the distinct prayer archetypes whom I meet with you at the synagogue. I describe below how those three exceptional rabbis, acting in their roles as a performer, a priest and a scribe, contributed significantly to my understanding of the spiritual landscape of the synagogue. I'll talk about a fourth famous activist rabbi when I describe the celebrity-monotheist model. And, yes, I'll also speak about myself, yet another rabbi, throughout this book.

Timeless Prayers

Another thing I do not dwell on in this book is to tell you about the origins of the prayers. Why? First off, it's difficult or impossible to tell when most prayers started and who started them. A real crucial characteristic of any prayer is to make it appear to you to be a timeless tradition, with no beginnings. And, anyhow, even if I tell you of some important cultural practice's origins—for instance, that baseball was invented by Abner Doubleday in Cooperstown, New York in 1839—how does that help you understand the game?

And, as you may know, that simple, recent fact about the origin of the game of baseball is highly disputed. The Doubleday-origin story is thought by many to be part of the sport's mythology. Jeff Idelson of the Baseball Hall of Fame in Cooperstown, New York has said about the sport's origin, "Baseball wasn't really born anywhere." He means to say that the game evolved over a long time, that baseball has no single, discoverable point of origin.

And so, returning to our main subject, it's legitimate to ask: How can I speak with any certainty about the origins of Jewish prayers, events shrouded in much greater mystery than baseball and that occurred up to 2000 or more years ago? We know only that the practices of the synagogue evolved over a long period of time and that they were influenced by many competing forces of history, society and culture.

But, just as baseball historians continue to repeat the mythological origin account of the sport, I report the origin narratives of the various prayers in brief at the proper times later in the book. Don't get all excited though. Here is a sample of what we have to offer.

Rabbi Jeremiah (fourth century) says (Yerushalmi Berakhot 4d) in reference to the origin of the Amidah prayer that "One-hundred-twenty elders, including about eighty prophets, instituted these prayers." These one-hundred-twenty elders are taken to be the men of an obscure group called the Great Assembly.

Another source (Talmud Bavli Megillah 17b) has a parallel of Rabbi Jeremiah's teaching about the origin of the liturgy: "Rabbi Yohanan said that, according to some, a baraita taught that one-hundred-twenty elders, including some prophets, instituted the Shemoneh Esreh (i.e., the Amidah, the Eighteen Blessings)." Another rabbinic text links the beginnings of the Amidah to a later authority, Simeon Hapaqoli, who formulated the blessings under the supervision of Gamaliel, the patriarch at Yavneh in Israel in the second century.

These traditional origin accounts do not tell a vivid or dramatic story. Overall, there is not much origin-folklore for the classical Jewish prayers. Baseball fares a little better in that department.

Imperfect Classifications

To explain what goes on in the synagogue, some people are satisfied to say that the four basic kinds of prayers are Wow! Oops! Gimme! and Thanks!, as described in a popular article, "The Right Way to Pray?" by Zev Chafetz in *The New York Times Magazine* (Sept. 16, 2009).

Rabbi Marc Gellman says in that article, "Wow! are prayers of praise and wonder at the creation. Oops! is asking for forgiveness. Gimme! is a request or a petition. Thanks! is expressing gratitude. That's the entire Judeo-Christian doxology. That's what we teach our kids in religious school."

I don't find that interpretive approach very helpful, I guess, because I'm not a kid in religious school. Not that it is wrong. There are prayers that fall into those four broad categories. But it's not enough to stop there and think we have decoded the liturgy in any substantial way. I say "thanks" to theories like those that Gellman provides, "wow" they really make me stop and think, but "oops" I need you to "gimme" more. What goes on in the synagogue is way more interesting and way more complex.

How can I get this point across? Let me try this comparison. The sport of golf is reducible to these four actions: driving off the tee, long-iron shots from the fairway, the short game around the green, and putting. But that analysis, though correct, tells you next to nothing about how to play the game or even how to watch the sport.

Or consider this comparison. I used to say about opera that I observed the difference between Italian, German and French operas: that the Italian ones are about love, war and love; the German are about war, love and war; and the French are about love, love and love.

Now that attempt at cleverness even may be true to some small degree. But, other than suggesting a funny typology, it tells us not much of substance about how to perform or how to appreciate the drama and emotion of any specific opera.

Gellman's four types tell us, at the most basic level, how people imagine that some prayers function to formulate a message sent from a praying supplicant to a listening deity. They don't tell us anything helpful or interesting about any specific prayer, Jewish or otherwise.

And the categorization fails to work dramatically and immediately if you enter an actual synagogue, look around, and start to try to characterize what is going on there. If you observe, to start with, the best-known Jewish liturgy, the Shema prayer, you find that it fits none of those categories. "Hear O, Israel, the Lord is our God. The Lord is one. And you shall love the Lord your God with all your heart, with all your soul, with all your might…" That does not conform to the Gellman typology. Oops! Then, if you look at the Torah readings in the synagogue, a major habitual activity in the services, well, that is something else, also not covered by the four-part typology. *Oops!*

Sure, I do want to find out in detail how the utterances of praise, petition or thanksgiving work in Judaism. Where do their words come from? What is the style and personality behind them? What is on the lists—in the contents of these big, general buckets of prayers?

And I need to examine all the rest of what Jews do in the synagogue to see the richness of expression and action beyond those four special cases of prayer. Those four types do not—as Gellman asserts—capture "the entire Judeo-Christian doxology." I don't really understand that claim anyway. Indeed, the term "doxology" means only praise, "A hymn or verse of praise to God." Am I confused by the Gellman approach? Yes, because, there is much more for me to do to get an understanding of the actual contents of Jewish prayers.

To dig into all of this, I need first to parse with you the sources of Jewish prayers. And we all can easily see by opening the prayer book, by listening to any service, that the Bible is the main source of much of what the performer presents in the synagogue. That is discovery number one in our quest to find the ideal synagogue—and God's favorite prayers—as we turn to the next chapter.

The Performer's Prayers

TO·RAH
[**toh**-*ruh*, **tawr**-*uh*; *Seph. Heb.* toh-**Rah**; *Ashk. Heb.* **toh**-R*uh*, **toi**-R*uh*]
—*noun* (*sometimes lowercase*)
1. the Pentateuch, being the first of the three Jewish divisions of the Old Testament. Compare *Tanach.*
2. a parchment scroll on which the Pentateuch is written, used in synagogue services.
3. the entire body of Jewish religious literature, law, and teaching as contained chiefly in the Old Testament and the Talmud.
4. law or instruction.

TA·NACH
[tah-**nah**KH]
—*noun* Hebrew.
the three Jewish divisions of the Old Testament, comprising the Law or Torah, the Prophets or *Neviim,* and the Hagiographa or *Ketuvim,* taken as a whole.

—Random House Dictionary, 2010

Artist, Poet, Musician

Cantor Louis Danto was a happy *hazzan.* His chanting was upbeat and peppy. I often heard him chant the synagogue services at the Atlantic Beach Jewish Center when I was a child and teenager in the 1950s and 60s. Just by listening to him I knew then that Danto was a world-class singer, a tenor whose beautiful voice was trained and ethereal. And I could see that he comprehended and loved the words of the prayers and cherished their meanings. I did not know at the time that he had studied at Talmudic yeshivas and in musical conservatories in Europe, and that he had won prizes for his talents. I could not have known that he would go on to perform worldwide, to record many albums of Jewish songs, of folk, popular, romantic and operatic music.

As a boy in Atlantic Beach, I could not foretell that this leader of our prayers years hence would be celebrated for his unmatched graceful yet ornate bel canto artistry, for his classical vocalization and for his just plain beautiful singing. I did recognize that I loved his extraordinary rendition of the *Shehecheyanu* blessing after the Kiddush on a Yom Tov holiday. In it, we praise God for keeping us alive and bringing us to a special sacred time. His blessing rang out with such emotion and expressivity that it just lifted my soul. I can recall vividly—and to this day—Danto's ringing repeated conclusion of the blessing, "*Lazman hazeh, lazman hazeh...*" which means, "...to this time, to this time." And I've tried at every holiday to replicate the joy of that singing as best as I can in my own chanting of the same blessing.

Danto defined for me an ideal—how a formal *davening* should sound. Wow, he set the bar way high up! His lyrical singing always changed the very character of the sanctuary. From listening to him, I learned that a good *hazzan* like Danto creates a palpable focus, a presence, a joyous, numinous, holy quality in the house of prayer.

Not every congregation can be fortunate enough to have such a performer. Many synagogues still do have professional cantors who lead the services. However, many congregations these days send up basically untrained volunteers to lead the public prayers.

Whatever the style, at every service in an actual brick-and-mortar synagogue, Jewish prayer is an orchestrated performance, led by a leader and joined by a congregation. The synagogue members attending the service act at times as a performing chorus and at other times as a listening audience.

Now, for your information, I'm postulating in this book that we speak mostly about prayer in a synagogue. To be precise though, Judaism does not require that you attend a community synagogue to engage in sanctioned, legitimate, effective prayer. You can pray alone, at home, or anywhere clean and proper. When a solitary Jew recites the synagogue prayers in private, it still can be a complex and moving performance. But by him or herself, the individual at prayer must play all the parts that I will identify here, serving as the leader, the chorus and the audience.

And so, without further adieu, please allow me to more formally introduce to you my first archetype, the performer.

This persona is in parts an artist, a poet and a musician. Performers play several roles in the synagogue. These, enumerated below, are the major troupe members, the group of actors, the cast that you will find in the synagogue, and a capsule introduction to each of their roles.

Dramatis Personæ Synagogæ

Hazzan. It's obvious that we may apply the label, performer, to an accomplished *hazzan*, a cantor. He leads the services from the designated places for leaders, the *bimah* in the center, or the *amud* in the front of the synagogue.

At the least, the *hazzan* has to be a master of the basic *nusach* and *niggun* of the synagogue, that is, the words of the prayers, their traditional tunes and how they must be performed in the services.

Chorus of the Congregation. The congregation actively participates in the services of the synagogue. So that makes them performers, too, although the intensity of their involvement varies from one instance of prayer to another.

Torah Reader. The Torah is read from the *bimah* in the center of the sanctuary. On Sabbaths and festivals, it is read in the middle of the service, after the morning prayers and before the additional prayers. It's easy to see that the reading of the Torah is central to the synagogue performance.

"Torah Reader" is also a part that *everyone* in the community gets to play at least one time. For the rite of passage for coming of age, the Bar Mitzvah Boy and the Bat Mitzvah Girl (except in most of the Orthodox community) must prepare for and play this role of Torah Reader. For the occasion, the young boy or girl usually will study and prepare to read a portion from the Torah in the synagogue on (or near) his or her coming-of-age birthday.

Kohanim. These important players, the priests, are direct descendants of Aaron, the brother of Moses, the original priests who served in the Tabernacle and the Temple. In the synagogue, they are given today a few mostly figurehead honors. On the holidays, during the Additional Service, they go up before the congregation, raise their hands and recite the three verses of the biblical priestly blessings. (Just to alert you, later in this book I use the term "priest" to describe an archetype of a style of prayer which is related to, but independent of, actual family ties and roles of this cast member.)

The *Shofar* Blower. This instrumental soloist plays the only musical instrument of the synagogue services. And, to be accurate, the *shofar* doesn't produce much of a tune. The ram's horn is blown on Rosh Hashanah, more as an alarm or call to arms, or a symbol of God's revelation at Sinai, than as a musical performance.

Now, what is the nature of the performances of all of these players? This archetype chants from his hymnal and sings his prayers using popular standard tunes—*nusach, niggun* and *trop,* the words, the tunes and cantillation notes—all essential parts of the text and of the performance of Jewish prayer. But, to know the performer, one must know more details about the gist and the genre of his or her performances.

What the performer performs in the *davening* in the synagogue in large part is from the Bible. So we must comprehend better the main ways that the Bible serves as a source of Jewish synagogue prayers.

Bible portions are performed as Bible. In this mode, the performer reads scripture qua scripture. Examples: (a) We take the Torah scroll out of the ark and readers read from it from the *bimah* in the center of the synagogue. (b) We take out a book of the prophets (usually in print, sometimes as a scroll) and readers read from it from the *bimah* in the center of the synagogue. (c) On holidays, we take out a book of the Writings, such as the book of Esther—the Megillah—on Purim and readers read from it from the *bimah.*

Bible sections are performed as prayers. In this mode, the performer plucks long blocks of text out of scripture and uses them as independent new liturgies of their own. Examples: (a) We read chapters from the Torah as part of core Jewish prayers, such as the Shema made up of chapters from the books of Deuteronomy and Numbers. (b) We read complete chapters from the Psalms as prayers of thanksgiving in the Hallel on festivals and elsewhere in the services daily.

Bible materials are extracted and interwoven into prayers. In this mode, the performer draws on scripture by making allusions to phrases, verses, ideas and incidents to formulate original composite liturgies, medleys, miscellanies and olios of biblical matter. Examples: (a) We combine or interject one or more biblical verses within various prayers. (b) We take phrases or make allusions to biblical words or phrases within different prayers.

Prayer is independent, without reference to the Bible. In this mode, we recite completely independent prayers that contain no identifiable words or concepts from the Bible.

A tacit premise of all of this performance is that God likes to hear his inspired Bible recited and chanted back to him. The performer uses the pre-existing received scripture in the liturgy of the synagogue extensively in the several manners I've described. These modes of prayers of the performer are woven together to make up most of what goes on in any synagogue. It is fair, then, to say that the Bible is a big component of God's favorite prayers.

From the perspective of the worshipper, another way to look at the role of the Bible as prayer is this. Some recitals, both in the worlds of music and the separate universe of prayer, will combine performances of original numbers and of classical numbers or *golden oldies*. That is also the case in the performances of prayers in the synagogue. The impresarios of all kinds of performances across the spectrum of music and art, from rock festivals to the Metropolitan Opera, throughout their calendar draw respectfully on their received body of recognized or classical works for beloved and reverent performances. So, too, does the performer archetype in our liturgical *minyan* turn for the contents of his performance to his inherited authoritative repertoire, to his scripts of religious contents that we call scripture.

I find it useful to categorize how the Bible is used in the synagogue as I outlined above and to give additional names to the major modes used by the performer for incorporating scripture into the public services of the synagogue. I call the first two categories (#1 and #2) the *comprehensive-Bible* modes and I label the third (#3) the *selective-Bible* mode.

To digress briefly, various writers in an anthology edited by James Kugel (*Prayers that Cite Scripture,* Cambridge, Mass., Harvard University Center for Jewish Studies, 2006), discuss a process that they call the "scripturalization" of the liturgy. These writers speculate that there once was a non-scripturalized Jewish liturgy, services without Bible passages, and then over time passages, verses and phrases from the Bible were put into it.

I don't agree with this perspective at all. I see the prayer book that we have in Judaism as the result of the "liturgization" of the Bible, meaning, the prayer composers in the great majority of instances started from the Bible. They sliced it, diced it and baked it into a liturgical pie. I prefer to say then with some certainty that the prayer book in essence is a large selection of the contents from the Bible that was transformed into a diverse set of practices for various styles of worship in the synagogue.

To return to my main discussion, let's examine some of the details and complexities of both of these methods of drawing the respected sacred texts into the recitals of the synagogue, the *comprehensive-Bible* mode and the *selective-Bible* mode. Let's consider some examples and explain a few of the rules and principles that determine how they work.

To know the performer in the *comprehensive-Bible* mode I look directly to the Torah service—the prescribed serial reading of the Five Books of Moses, the Pentateuch, within the services (#1).

For many people this mode of synagogue performance is notable or memorable—as I noted—because it's associated with the Jewish rite of passage of boys and girls into adulthood. If you had a bar mitzvah or a bat mitzvah, you know that it probably meant you had to learn to chant a short Torah portion, called a *maftir*, and a selection from the prophets, called a *haftorah*. Sometimes the boy or girl chants more of the Torah portion and sometimes, none of it at all, singing only the blessings before and after and letting a professional reader chant the actual the biblical verses. Even if you haven't performed this ritual yourself, you likely have attended the bar or bat mitzvah of a friend or relative or perhaps you've seen the chanting in a Hollywood movie or on a TV show episode.

The Torah reading-service is performed in the synagogue every week. Over a span of either one or three years in a predetermined and fixed liturgical schedule, the entire Torah is chanted.

Now you may ask a fair question: Is this liturgy or lectionary? The answer is that the Torah is chanted and not taught in the synagogue. It is liturgy, but a rich and informative form of prayer. It is a course of Jewish beliefs performed in liturgical chants.

I used to tell my students that the one secret to mastering the materials of a course was to read the textbook. And if the book was difficult and they did not at first understand it, I suggested that they read it aloud to their roommate or friend.

The Torah service is a most effective and persistent means of transmitting the course materials of Judaism to the students in the synagogue. Here is how it is carried out.

In the annual cycle variant, which is practiced today in most houses of worship, the performer reads the entire Five Books of Moses over the course of a year—broken down over a period of fifty-four weekly readings—generally one *parasha* for every Sabbath. The first part of each portion is read as a sort of preview in the morning services of the synagogue on Mondays and Thursdays and on in the afternoons on Saturdays. On Saturday morning, selected Torah passages, called *maftir*, are read again.

There are some one-hundred Bible chapters from the prophets that are read in conjunction with the Torah readings. Each one is called a *Haftarah*. All of this constitutes the annual cycle, which has been commonly practiced since the Middle Ages. In earlier times, a more drawn out and less intensive Torah cycle, completed over a three-year period, was practiced in the synagogue. There were, according to various counts, 141, 154, or 167 *parasha* divisions in the triennial cycle that was practiced in antiquity.

The result, in any case, is that the whole Torah—the Five Books of Moses, also known as the Pentateuch—is read in the synagogue on a one- or three-year cycle. That tells us something both obvious and significant, namely that at the core of rabbinic Judaism is the veneration of the Torah as its sacred constitution. The public ceremonial *liturgical* reading of Bible passages in the synagogue is the most visible and culturally significant way that Jewish communities worldwide act out that value.

But I do need to note that the content that is read changes every week. In the existing models of chanting that I just described, Jews chant most of the Torah's passages in public either once annually or once every three years. Compared to other prayers of the synagogue, this Torah service is not an exceedingly repetitive ritual practice.

Contrast this schedule of Bible readings with the more frequently recited prayers. The content of those never changes. The same set of Sabbath prayers are repeated fifty times, that is once every week of the year. Some of the daily prayers are repeated even more frequently, up to three times a day—over one-thousand times each year—as is the case of the Amidah and the Aleinu, prayers we shall address directly in later chapters.

The frequency of repeated identical recitations may actually tell us little about the relative importance of the components of the service. Both the Bible readings and the other prayers are crucial to defining the content of Judaism, but because the latter are more recurrent, they appear to be more prominent and more pronounced in the synagogue services.

Accordingly, to sum it up, the most basic ritual way that the liturgy evinces the *comprehensive-Bible* use of prior texts is in these actions: the weekly Torah service, the prophetic *haftarot*, and the festival recitation of the Five *Megillot* where the designated books of the canon are read in a ritualized public context.

The Torah is read in the synagogue straight through from its beginning in Genesis through its end in Deuteronomy, in order and without abridgement or selection. The prophets are not read in that fashion. Each week, a selection of a prophetic passage accompanies the weekly Torah reading. The principle that governs why synagogue authorities selected a prophetic passage appears to be some simple associative elements of a prophetic theme in common with a Torah theme. The chanting of the passages from the prophets does not present to the synagogue from those books any systematic religious value or unifying theological world view. In contrast to the Torah, the Jew in the synagogue does not hear the Prophets or Writings in straight order without abridgement.

The bottom line is that, even given the extent of the scriptural materials recited publicly, the majority of the contents of the second and third divisions of the Tanakh (Torah, Neviim, Ketuvim, what we call the Hebrew Bible, namely the divisions of the Prophets—Neviim— and the Writings—Ketuvim) are not prescribed for reading in the public liturgy of the synagogue.

As I mentioned just above, another part of the *comprehensive* use of scripture is the chanting of the five scrolls of diverse content and origins, primary readings from the Ketuvim. These Bible books are intoned in full annually in the synagogue on this schedule: Esther on Purim, Lamentations on the Ninth of Av, Song of Songs on Passover, Ruth on Shavuot, and Qohelet (Ecclesiastes) on Sukkot. One entire book of the Minor Prophets, Jonah, is read on Yom Kippur at the Minhah afternoon service.

In these six biblical scrolls that are chanted annually, we bring into the synagogue a variety of literary and cultural biblical archetypes. Specifically, these books present to the public stories and poems of various Israelite women characters from the Song of Songs, Esther and Ruth. Other readings introduce into the mix the personality of the victims of destruction and exile speaking out in the book of Lamentations, intoned on the Ninth of Av. We also hear of a narrative of a heroic religious archetype of sorts in the book of Jonah, which is chanted on Yom Kippur.

Finally, there are several dozen or so complete Psalms (from the third division of the Tanakh, the *Ketuvim*) that also fall under the rubric of the *comprehensive* use of scripture in Jewish liturgy. These hymns are recited as part of the regular cycle of prayers. I have illustrated this in my chart outlining the morning services, which you can find online at www.godsfavoriteprayers.com.

It should be clear that there is a lot of Bible chanting going on in all synagogues. In some synagogues, all of this chanting is done by a regular professional employee, called a *hazzan,* a *shammash* or a *shaliach tzibbur* for the prayers and by a *baal koreh,* a trained reader, for the extended Torah portions. In many other, less formal synagogues lay people volunteer or are called upon to lead the services on an ad hoc basis.

In the abstract, it makes little difference who actually performs the singing and chanting. That person is for us simply our performing artist. The archetype who chants or intones the designated extended Bible passages in the synagogue acts much like the opera star who performs the libretto of his classic works or the rock star who stages his signature pieces.

Bear this in mind as I move on to present my next mode or process, the *selective-Bible* mode. This is a more intricate use of scripture in liturgy. Over the centuries, a host of often unknown and anonymous authors of liturgy—artist-poet-musician-prayer-writers—interlaced biblical phrases, verses and chapters in the more frequent synagogue services, daily or weekly. The authors of the major prayers across the board chose to mine scripture and embed selective contents from the Bible into their own originally written texts of prayers.

Biblical verses were liberally employed and interspersed within the original standardized daily morning liturgy and the services for the Sabbath and festivals that were written by the ancient rabbis. The results of those creative processes in turn tell us about the social and cosmic visions of Judaism and its theology as conceived of by these artist-poet-musician shapers of that liturgy.

You may notice that I deliberately blur the lines here between the original shaper of the liturgy and the performer of the services. For the most part, as I suggested previously, we don't have much specific information about who selected the verses and created the composite prayers. And, for a person trying to find spiritual meaning in the synagogue, it is the performer who brings the prayers to life. Their origins don't much come into play.

As you no doubt have noticed, I have met in my synagogue both creative types whom I call the artist-poet-musicians, and the performers of their many impressive liturgical compositions that comprise major parts of the synagogue service.

These creative works—the *selective-Bible* mode prayers— are discourses, poems and other treatments of great religious themes. Later, I associate some of these works with more distinctive voices that I attribute to individual models, which I call a scribe or a priest, a mystic, a meditator or a celebrity.

For now, to understand the present archetype better, let me consider one especially elegant and detailed example of a liturgical piece that shows what an artist-poet-musician can elegantly do to form an expressive holiday liturgy primarily using the *selective-Bible* mode of his expression.

That simply means that the artist-poet-musician takes a variety of Bible verses from different places and puts them together to make a new prayer. Among those prominent prayer compositions that were constructed from carefully chosen biblical materials is the Musaf Amidah for Rosh Hashanah—a beautiful composite that sets forth in praise of God, the prominent theological ideas for the New Year. It is an especially dramatic performance in the synagogue because, during its recitation on the great festival of awe, the *shofar* is blown. The use of any instrument or prop is especially rare in the otherwise spartan services of the synagogue rite. Hence the *shofar* performance underlines the special nature of the day and highlights the liturgy that surrounds it.

In the Rosh Hashanah Additional Service, this composite, three-part liturgy accompanies the sounding of the ram's horn. The sections of that prayer are embedded in the festival Amidah and are given names according to their thematic contents—first "Malchiyot—Kingships," then "Zichronot—Remembrances" and finally "Shofrot—Horn Blasts." These segments deal respectively with great subjects of the holiday: God's kingship, God's covenants with the forefathers and God's revelation of the Torah to the children of Israel.

The writer of these special prayers was an anonymous ancient and great artist-poet-musician of the Talmudic era who selected and wove together ten biblical verses as discourses for each of the three theological themes of the holy day. After each segment is recited, a designated performer blows the *shofar*. Hence, the religious meaning of the artist's lyrics expanded on the ritual music of the ram's horn and gave to the stark sounds some framing words. The biblical verses are the textual contents, the libretto or lyrics of the New Year performance. The *shofar* blasts serve as the musical accompaniment, the punctuation for these prayers following the chant.

It's a bit ironic to note that there is a bon mot about the *shofar* attributed to a great rabbinic figure of the past century, Rabbi Saul Lieberman. Lieberman called the blowing of the *shofar* in the synagogue on Rosh Hashanah, "a prayer without words." I guess, to be fair to him, he meant that if you isolate the *shofar* sounds and look at them on their own, they too could be considered a prayer in one sense of the term. I find it amusing, though, to think that anyone who has been to *shul* on the New Year, in particular a rabbi of note, would say that the *shofar* sounds ought to be thought of "without words" extracted from their context. At the very least, the blowing of the *shofar* has to be appreciated in those accompanying passages of a great, great many words. In the bigger scheme of the holiday liturgy, the sounding of the *shofar* is a solo instrumental interlude inextricably embedded within a dramatic, somber performance of 1000 actual pages of prayers, indeed with all the words of the holiday *Machzor*.

Remarkably, considering the number of books that have been written by rabbis on the Bible and the Talmud, there is comparatively little rabbinic commentary on the prayer book. Some years ago, I was fortunate to hear my teacher, Rabbi Joseph Soloveitchik, expound in a lecture on the significance of the thirty-some verses that were chosen for the discourse as the textual accompaniment of the *shofar's* spare music.

The Master Performer

Let me give some background about my mentor, Rabbi Soloveitchik. His followers extolled him with a reverent nickname. They called him the *Rav*, simply the Master. I consider the Rav to be a master performer par excellence of the synagogue liturgy (when on occasion he led the services), a great pedagogue in the classroom, a scholar of note and interpreter of the substance of the performances of the synagogue. And finally, he was an amazing beginner.

In my family, we venerated the Rav above all other rabbis. We spoke of him with the utmost reverence that one would bestow only upon a truly saintly man. And he was one of the great Orthodox rabbis of the twentieth century. He was born into a rabbinic family in Eastern Europe. After mastering all of rabbinic literature, he studied philosophy at the University in Berlin. He was known not just as a rabbi but also as a *Gadol*—a title reserved for person of the greatest stature in Torah learning and highest authority in Jewish religious matters.

As a Yeshiva College senior, I started four years of learning in Rabbi Soloveitchik's Talmud *shiur*. In my three post-graduate years of study with the Rav, I earned my ordination and became a rabbi.

I received in those four years so much from the Rav: a methodology of learning the Talmud, a theology of Judaism grounded in philosophy, and some secrets of exceptional pedagogy.

Let me expand on this last point. The Rav would sometimes, in an occasional moment of gently deprecating and surprising self-reflection, refer to himself as a *poshutte melamed,* the Yiddish description of a simple teacher of beginners. That statement puzzled me. Surely the Rav was the greatest Orthodox Talmudic sage of his generation. How could he represent himself in this ordinary way?

One day, I accidentally discovered what he might have meant. We rabbinical students convened at the fourth floor of the college building in an oversized classroom for our *shiur,* to begin studying a famous Talmud passage that was a discourse about the laws in Tractate Shabbat. That day, I was using a Talmud volume from a small, bound set that my uncle Rabbi Noah Goldstein had used when he studied in the Rav's *shiur.* I found interleaved in this hand-me-down book a page of my uncle's notes from the Rav's discourse on this same Talmud passage, fifteen or twenty years earlier.

As we started reading the text, the Rav sat at his desk at the front of the class, as usual, with books of the Talmud arrayed all around him. He opened to the page for the day and began to perform the pedagogic magic in which he was so skilled. He started the class: "All right. Where were we?" He made it seem to us all as if he was looking at the text for the very first time. He made every question he raised appear as if he was discovering a problem afresh. Every answer and each explanation that he examined in the medieval commentators, Rashi or the Tosafot, he made appear to us as if it were new to him—a complete surprise.

Over the course of a class that lasted more than two hours, the Rav dramatically unfolded a complex and intricate exposition of the *sugya,* the text and its topic—and each stage of the discourse seemed so original and alive. Yet, as I followed along and read my uncle's notes, I saw that the Rav was repeating—in order—each and every element of the *shiur* exactly as he had given it years before, insight by insight, question by question and answer by answer. He had all of us students in the room convinced that he had just newly discovered every element of his learning. Yet I had proof in front of me to the contrary.

I saw that day how the Rav had the ability to make every act of learning a new, exciting and living revelation. I have striven to emulate him ever since, to replicate this ability and to achieve as a learner and as a teacher some small element of this revelation.

Hanging over my desk where I write, I have a quotation from the great German poet Rainer Maria Rilke, "If the angel deigns to come it will be because you have convinced her not by tears but by your humble resolve to be always beginning: to be a beginner." I believe the Rav echoed that sentiment in his teaching and learning and, certainly, in his praying.

The Rav's ability to find the freshness in learning and in praying inspires this book. In part, in this extended discourse, I try to present content for fresh solutions to the frustrating issue of how to escape the monotony of the repetitive rituals of prayer. Indeed, it is a challenge to rediscover meaning and insight continually within the routine. It's easier said than done—to be a beginner.

I try here in this volume to present as new my humble discoveries of voices and personalities in the prayer book to satisfy my own need to find what is fresh in what I repeat daily, weekly and annually. And in the spirit of my teacher the Rav, I aspire throughout this volume to provide you, the reader, with insights that will allow you to discover your own ways to always be a simple beginner in the appreciation and practice of your own praying.

To help us appreciate an important representative example of the expression of the artist-poet-musician archetype in the synagogue services, I now turn to a sample of the Rav's comments on a few of our liturgy texts.

A *Shofar* Opera Libretto

Here, then, is the traditional libretto of a *shofar* opera in three acts. These texts are more familiarly known as the foundational High Holiday prayers in the Musaf Amidah. I interleave into the prayers below a selection of a few basic examples of the insights that the Rav and other interpreters of the past have taught about the Rosh Hashanah Additional Service.

In fact, this is not a complicated section of the Jewish liturgy. To expand on what I said just above, the Kingship-

Covenant-Revelation liturgy—Malchiyot, Zichronot and Shofrot—accompanies the sounding of the ram's horn in the additional service on Rosh Hashanah, as follows.

<u>Act 1</u>: The prayer opens with the Aleinu, a text that characterizes the dramatic archetype whom I call in this book the celebrity-monotheist.

Historians of the liturgy believe that the Aleinu originally found its way into Jewish prayer as this inaugural segment of the Malchiyot—Kingship prayers. Later, it was appropriated into the daily prayers and became the closing liturgy of every service.

In this Rosh Hashanah context, the Aleinu announces the theme of God the King and the section after it provides us with our first set of selected biblical passages:

> It is our duty to praise the Lord of all things, to ascribe greatness to him who formed the world in the beginning, since he has not made us like the nations of other lands, and has not placed us like other families of the earth, since he has not assigned unto us a portion as unto them, nor a lot as unto all their multitude. For we bend the knee and offer worship and thanks before the supreme King of kings, the Holy One, blessed be he, who stretched forth the heavens and laid the foundations of the earth, the seat of whose glory is in the heavens above, and the abode of whose might is in the loftiest heights. He is our God; there is none else: in truth he is our King; there is none besides him; as it is written in his Torah, "And you shall know this day, and lay it to your heart, that the Lord he is God in heaven above and upon the earth beneath: there is none else."

> We therefore hope in you, O Lord our God, that we may speedily behold the glory of your might, when you will remove the abominations from the earth, and the idols will be utterly cut off, when the world will be perfected under the kingdom of the Almighty, and all the children of flesh will call upon your name, when you will turn unto yourself all the wicked of the earth. Let all the inhabitants of the world perceive and know that unto you every knee must bow, every tongue must swear. Before you, O Lord our God, let them bow and fall; and unto your glorious name let them give honor; let them all accept the yoke of your kingdom,

and do you reign over them speedily, and forever and ever. For the kingdom is yours, and to all eternity you will reign in glory.

The theme of the Aleinu announced above is that God is King, he is One, there is no other and that all the peoples of the earth will come to acknowledge that. I will explain at length below, in the chapter called "The Celebrity's Prayers," that this prayer speaks for a particular archetype of the synagogue. The viewpoint and personality it communicates believes in the coming of an age of struggle that will see the ultimate victory of the Israelite people over all the nations, of the Lord over all the contending gods.

And, now, let us see how the liturgy writer makes the ten assembled verses that follow in the New Year prayer try to articulate this theme.

The Rav observed that the verses, as we shall now see, are drawn first from the Torah, then from the Writings, then from the prophets. He asked why this is so, considering that the canonical Tanakh, the Hebrew Bible as we have it today, is ordered Torah, Neviim (Prophets) and Ketuvim (Writings). To answer, he says simply that the prayer writer wanted to address God's actions in chronological order, past (as found in the Torah), present (as found in the Writings) and future (as foretold in the Prophets).

The first three verses from the Torah do not express the complete idea of the liturgy. In fact, the idea of a King-God triumphing over other gods and the coming of an ultimate era where all peoples will worship him is not found in the Torah. Instead, the verses pick texts that have echoes of God called "King" or of his "reign."

> [1] As it is written in your Torah, "The Lord shall reign forever and ever (Exodus 15:18)."
> [2] And it is said, "He has not beheld iniquity in Jacob, neither has he seen perverseness in Israel: the Lord his God is with him, and the trumpet shout of a King is among them (Numbers 23:31)."
> [3] And it is said, "And he became King in Yeshurun, when the heads of the people were gathered, the tribes of Israel together (Deuteronomy 33:5)."

The next three verses from the Writings do express more of the ideas of the complete narrative embedded in the liturgy. In fact, the idea of a King-God ruling over other nations is a present theme in the Psalms. Yet the story of the coming of an ultimate era where all peoples will worship God is not found there. The verses again pick texts with echoes of God called "King" or of his "reign."

> [4] And in your Ketuvim it is written, saying, "For the kingdom is the Lord's, and he is ruler over the nations (Psalms 22:29)."
>
> [5] And it is said, "The Lord reigns; he has robed him in majesty; the Lord has robed him, yea, he has girded himself with strength: the world also is set firm; that it cannot be moved (Psalms 93:1)."
>
> [6] And it is said, "Lift up your heads, O you gates, and be you lifted up, you everlasting doors, that the King of glory may come in. Who, then, is the King of glory? The Lord, strong and mighty, the Lord mighty in battle. Lift up your heads, O you gates; yea, lift them up, you everlasting doors, that the King of glory may come in. Who, then, is the King of glory? The Lord of hosts, he is the King of glory. (Selah.) (Psalms 44:7-10)"

The last of the Psalms citation is actually four verses. The Rav notes that they express a single kingship theme, a "challenge to humanity to voluntarily recognize the dominion of God."

The next set of three verses is from the Prophets. They do express the complete idea of the liturgy because the idea of a King-God triumphing over other gods and the coming of an ultimate era where all peoples will worship him is derived from the prophetic works of ancient Israel. The verses from the books of Isaiah, Obadiah and Zechariah directly support the notion of the ultimate triumph of our one true God over the others after a day and time of judgment over the nations of the earth.

> [7] And by the hands of your servants, the prophets, it is written, saying, "Thus says the Lord, the King of Israel and his Redeemer, the Lord of hosts: I am the first, and I am the last; and beside me there is no God (Isaiah 44:16)."

[8] And it is said, "And saviors shall come up on Mount Zion to judge the Mount of Esau, and the kingdom shall be the Lord's (Obadiah 1:21)."

[9] And it is said, "And the Lord shall be King over all the earth: in that day shall the Lord be One and his name One (Zechariah 14:9)."

The final verse is again culled from the Torah, a bookend closing off the set of ten. It cites one of the best-known verses of the Torah and a centerpiece of the liturgy itself, the first verse of the Shema, Deuteronomy 6:4. That passage also does not express the complete idea of the liturgy because, while, in fact, it does declare the monotheistic unity of one God, it does not relate a struggle with the other deities or hint at a coming age when the oneness of God will be realized for the whole of the earth. For the purposes of this kingship liturgy, it appears to be enough that the verse declares God to be one. Specifying literally that God is King is not a necessary component for the inclusion of the verse.

[10] And in your Torah it is written saying, "Hear, O Israel: the Lord our God, the Lord is One (Deuteronomy 6:4)."

The Rav says that the tenth proof text verse in each of the three sections is part of the closing appeal of the liturgy. The first part concludes with a reiteration of the basics of the main story line, and a "request" that God will reveal his reign as king over all the earth. The closing petition of the prayer then continues:

Our God and God of our fathers, reign you in your glory over the whole universe, and be exalted above all the earth in your honor, and shine forth in the splendor and excellence of your might upon all the inhabitants of your world, that whatsoever has been made may know that you have made it, and whatsoever has been created may understand that you have created it, and whatsoever has breath in its nostrils may say, the Lord God of Israel is King and his dominion rules over all.

[Our God and God of our fathers, accept our rest.] Sanctify us by your commandments, and grant our portion in your Torah; satisfy us with your goodness, and gladden us with your salvation: [and in your love and favor, O Lord our God, let us inherit your holy Sabbath; and may Israel, who hallow your name, rest thereon]. O purify our hearts to serve you in truth, for you are God in truth, and your word is truth, and endures forever. Blessed are you, O Lord, King over all the earth, who sanctifies [the Sabbath and] Israel and the Day of Memorial.

[And then the *shofar* is blown.]

Act 2: The next theme of the Rosh Hashanah Musaf to be announced is Zichronot, that God remembers his covenants with Israel. This theological statement begins with a liturgy that states an underlying assumption of the High Holidays, namely that an all-knowing God will judge all nations and all individuals on this day, the day that he created the world. God also knows all the thoughts and merits of each individual and judges them. And then the prayer switches abruptly to Noah as the example of one man who was spared the harsh judgment brought upon the earth and whose covenant with God protects us from destruction:

> You remember what was wrought from eternity and are mindful of all that has been formed from of old: before you all secrets are revealed and the multitude of hidden things from the beginning; for there is no forgetfulness before the throne of your glory; nor is there anything hidden from your eyes. You remember every deed that has been done: not a creature is concealed from you: all things are manifest and known unto you, O Lord our God, who looks and sees to the end of all generations. For you will bring on the appointed time of memorial when every spirit and soul shall be visited, and the multitudinous works be remembered with the innumerable throng of your creatures.
>
> From the beginning you did make this your purpose known, and from aforetime you did disclose it. This day, on which was the beginning of your work, is a memorial of the first day, for it is a statute for Israel, a decree of the God of Jacob.
>
> Thereon also sentence is pronounced upon countries— which of them are destined to the sword and which to peace, which to famine and which to plenty; and each separate creature is visited thereon, and recorded for life or for death. Who is not visited on this day?

For the remembrance of every creature comes before you, each man's deeds and destiny, his works and ways, his thoughts and schemes, his imaginings and achievements.

Happy is the man who forgets you not, and the son of man who strengthens himself in you; for they that seek you shall never stumble, neither shall any be put to shame who trust in you. Yea, the remembrance of all works comes before you, and you enquire into the doings of them all.

Of Noah also you were mindful in your love, and did visit him with a promise of salvation and mercy, when you brought the waters of the flood to destroy all flesh on account of their evil deeds. So his remembrance came before you, O Lord our God, to increase his seed like the dust of the earth, and his offspring like the sand of the sea.

The Rav finds in the liturgy several themes. First, God's dominion over humankind crosses all of time from the beginning to the end of days. Second, God sees all and remembers all, every act of every individual. Third, God relates uniquely through the covenant to the Jewish people.

And, now, let us see how the liturgy writer makes the ten assembled verses in the prayer try to articulate the themes. The first three verses are from the Torah. They do not express the complete idea of the discursive liturgy but appear to focus on God remembering his covenants with Noah, and with Abraham, Isaac and Jacob.

[1] As it is written in your Torah, "And God remembered Noah, and every living thing, and all the cattle that were with him in the ark: and God made a wind to pass over the earth, and the waters subsided (Genesis 8:3)."

[2] And it is said, "And God heard their groaning, and God remembered his covenant with Abraham, with Isaac and with Jacob (Exodus 2:24)."

[3] And it is said, "Then will I remember my covenant with Jacob; and also my covenant with Isaac, and also my covenant with Abraham will I remember; and I will remember the land (Leviticus 26:42)."

The next three verses are from the Writings. They also do not express the full range of ideas of the introductory prayer. Each verse alludes to remembrance of a covenant:

[4] And in your Ketuvim it is written saying, "He has made a memorial for his wondrous works: the Lord is gracious and full of compassion (Psalms 91:4)."

[5] And it is said, "He has given food unto them that fear him: he will ever be mindful of his covenant (Psalms 91:5)."

[6] And it is said, "And he remembered for them his covenant, and repented according to the multitude of his loving-kindness (Psalms 106:45)."

The final set of three verses is from the Prophets. Again, each verse alludes to remembrance of a covenant:

[7] And by the hands of your servants, the prophets, it is written saying, "Go and cry in the ears of Jerusalem, saying, Thus says the Lord, I remember for you the kindness of your youth, the love of your bridal state; how you went after me in the wilderness, in a land that was not sown (Jeremiah 2:2)."

[8] And it is said, "Nevertheless, I will remember my covenant with you in the days of your youth, and I will establish unto you an everlasting covenant (Ezekiel 16:60)."

[9] And it is said, "Is Ephraim a precious son unto me? Is he a caressed child? As often as I spoke against him, I earnestly remembered him. Therefore my heart yearns for him: I will surely have mercy upon him, says the Lord (Jeremiah 31:20)."

The Rav develops a homily based on the choice and order of the three verses above. The first two promise that God will remember Israel as innocent and worthy, as young people who have not yet become corrupt. This is like a father's love, says the Rav. His compassion is aroused when he remembers when his children were young.

The nuance in the third verse is that Israel is depicted as though still a child. This is like a mother's love, says the Rav. A mother can always vividly see her children as her babies and thereby have compassion for them more immediately.

The last verse, below, is again culled from the Torah, a bookend closing off the set of ten drawn from a chapter in Leviticus where the idea of the covenants is treated in detail. The verse is embedded in the closing liturgical statement, at the end of the paragraph that evokes the dramatic covenant of the Torah that God made with Abraham at the binding of Isaac on Mount Moriah:

> Our God and God of our fathers, let us be remembered by you for good: grant us a visitation of salvation and mercy from your heavens, the heavens of old; and remember unto us, O Lord our God, the covenant and the loving-kindness and the oath which you swore unto Abraham our father on Mount Moriah: and may the binding with which Abraham our father bound his son Isaac on the altar appear before you how he overbore his compassion in order to perform your will with a perfect heart. So may your compassion overbear your anger against us; in your great goodness may the fierceness of your wrath turn aside from your people, your city and your inheritance.
>
> Fulfill unto us, O Lord our God, the word in which you have bidden us trust in your Torah through the hand of Moses your servant, from the mouth of your glory, [10] as it is said, "But I will remember unto them the covenant of their ancestors, whom I brought forth out of the land of Egypt in the sight of the nations, that I might be their God: I am the Lord" (Leviticus 26:45).
>
> For you are he who remembered from eternity all forgotten things, and before the throne of whose glory there is no forgetfulness. O remember the binding of Isaac this day in mercy unto his seed. Blessed are you, O Lord, who remembers the covenant.
>
> [And then the *shofar* is blown.]

Act 3: The final section, Shofarot, blasts of the horn, deals with the notions of God's revelations to Israel at Sinai. The Rav emphasized that Maimonides directly linked the *shofar* to repentance. Its sounds rouse the Jew from his slumber to recognize his sins and seek forgiveness. And recall that the *shofar* itself is bent, says the Rav. According to the Talmud, this symbolized a person humbly bent over in prayer.

> You did reveal yourself in a cloud of glory unto your holy people in order to speak with them. Out of heaven you did make them hear your voice and was revealed unto them in clouds of purity. The whole world trembled at your presence, and the works of creation were in awe of you, when you did thus reveal yourself, O our King, upon Mount

Sinai to teach your people the Torah and commandments, and did make them hear your majestic voice and your holy utterances out of flames of fire. Amidst thunders and lightning you did manifest yourself to them, and while the shofar sounded you did shine forth upon them.

The theme is clear and unambiguous. God revealed himself to Israel, and the *shofar* accompanied those events. The first three verses from the Torah spell this out:

[1] As it is written in your Torah, "And it came to pass on the third day, when it was morning, that there were thunders and lightning, and a thick cloud upon the mount, and the sound of the shofar exceedingly loud; and all the people that were in the camp trembled (Exodus 19:16)."

[2] And it is said, "And the sound of the shofar waxed louder and louder; Moses spoke, and God answered him by a voice (Exodus 19:19)."

[3] And it is said, "And all the people perceived the thundering and the lightning, and the sound of the shofar, and the mountain smoking: and when the people saw it, they were moved and stood afar off (Exodus 20:15)."

The next three verses from the Writings extend the theme of the prayer. The *shofar* is used in celebration and praise of the Lord, God the King. The set concludes with an added bonus set of verses from Psalms.

[4] And in your Ketuvim it is written, saying, "God is gone up with a shout, the Lord with the sound of a shofar (Psalms 47:16)."

[5] And it is said, "With trumpets and sound of shofar shout joyously before the King, the Lord (Psalms 98:6)."

[6] And it is said, "Blow the shofar on the new moon, at the beginning of the month, for our day of festival; for it is a statute for Israel, a decree of the God of Jacob (Psalms 81:45)."

[6a] And it is said, "Praise you the Lord. Praise God in his sanctuary: praise him in the firmament of his power. Praise him for his mighty acts: praise him according to his abundant greatness. Praise him with the blast of the shofar: praise him with the harp and the lyre. Praise him with the timbrel and dance: praise him with stringed instruments and the pipe. Praise him with the clear-toned cymbals:

praise him with the loud-sounding cymbals. Let everything that has breath praise the Lord. Praise you the Lord (Psalms 150)."

The Rav explains that the verses above describe how revelation from God is not confined just to a past event at Sinai and a future messianic time. A more subtle form of revelation is accessible in the present to every Jew who can experience God's presence and know that he is not alone. The Rav calls this need to find God in the here-and-now a "halakhic imperative"—a requirement of Jewish law. To pray properly, a person must feel he is in proximity to God.

The Rav adds that the last set of verses [6a] breaks the structure of the prayer. The verses are not just proof texts of the theological theme of the section. They are a burst of song in God's presence. The Jew today must visualize himself as if he was at the Temple in the days of old in the presence of God. And, hence, he needs to break out in song.

The last set of verses from the Prophets extends the message. The *shofar* is not just a sign of God's revelation to Israel. It heralds God's ultimate, universal revelation to all the nations of the earth. In this manner, the final section here serves as a bookend to the opening section of the first part of the liturgy above in Malchiyot, where God's dominion over the nations of the earth is announced.

> [7] And by the hands of your servants, the prophets, it is written saying, "All you inhabitants of the world, and you dwellers on the earth, when an ensign is lifted up on the mountains, see you, and when the shofar is blown, hear you (Isaiah 18:3)."
>
> [8] And it is said, "And it shall come to pass on that day, that a great shofar shall be blown; and they shall come who were lost in the land of Assyria, and they that were outcasts in the land of Egypt; and they shall worship the Lord in the holy mountain at Jerusalem (Isaiah 27:13)."
>
> [9] And it is said, "And the Lord shall be seen over them, and his arrow shall go forth as the lightning: and the Lord God shall blow the shofar, and shall go with the whirlwinds of the south. The Lord of hosts shall be a shield unto them (Zechariah 9:14)."
>
> So be a shield unto your people Israel with your peace.

> Our God and God of our fathers, sound the great shofar for our freedom, lift up the ensign to gather our exiles; bring our scattered ones among the nations near unto you, and gather our dispersed from the ends of the earth. Lead us with exultation unto Zion, your city, and unto Jerusalem the place of your sanctuary with everlasting joy; and there we will prepare before you the offerings that are obligatory for us.

And again, the last verse is culled from the Torah, and embedded in the concluding liturgy, and extends and associates the *shofar* with the sacrifices of the Tabernacle.

The Rav points out that [8] implies at the end of days that God himself will sound the *shofar*. Hence, this suggests that the revelation of the future in the age of the messiah will replicate that of the past when God revealed himself with the sound of a *shofar* at Mount Sinai.

> As is commanded us in your Torah through the hand of Moses your servant, from the mouth of your glory, [10] as it is said, "And in the day of your gladness, and in your set feasts, and in the beginnings of your months, you shall blow with the trumpets over your burnt offerings, and over the sacrifices of your peace offerings; and they shall be to you for a memorial before your God: I am the Lord your God" (Numbers 10:10).
>
> For you hear the sound of the shofar and give heed to the trumpet-blast, and there is none like unto you. Blessed are you, O Lord, who in mercy hears the sound of the trumpet-blast of your people Israel.
>
> [And then the *shofar* is blown.]

There's much more to be said about the theology and artistry of the prayers. My purpose is to show, through the liturgy of the dramatic central part of the Rosh Hashanah additional service, how the performer—the artist-poet-musician—weaves Bible verses together to create from many Bible-strands some elaborate liturgy-fabrics, the cloth of the expressions of synagogue prayers.

I discovered along my spiritual journeys that the other ideal people that I met in the synagogue took all of this biblical material and much more and performed it so as to express their inner—sometimes mystical—longings in accord with their distinctive, slightly otherworldly personalities, as we see on the next leg of our journey, when we meet the mystic and her prayers.

The Mystic's Prayers

KAD·DISH
[*Ashk. Heb.* **kah**-dish; *Seph. Heb.* kah-**deesh**]
—*noun, plural* Kad·di·shim
[*Ashk. Heb.* kah-**dish**-im; *Seph. Heb.* kah-dee-**sheem**].
Judaism.
1. (*italics*) a liturgical prayer, consisting of three or six verses, recited at specified points during each of the three daily services and on certain other occasions.
2. (*italics*) Also called Mourner's Kaddish. The five-verse form of this prayer that is recited at specified points during each of the three daily services by one observing the mourning period of 11 months, beginning on the day of burial, for a deceased parent, sibling, child, or spouse, and by one observing the anniversary of such a death.
3. Kaddishim, persons who recite this prayer.

—Random House Dictionary, 2010

In my spiritual quest in scores of synagogues, not surprisingly I sought after and expected to meet up with some mystical personalities. After all, mystical traditions are inextricably associated with the religions of the world.

Allow me introduce you to Hannah the mystic, one such ideal type whom I met. To do this, I first must take you way back to the earliest description in Tanakh of an individual reciting a prayer at a sacred shrine. The brief narrative from I Samuel chapter 1 tells us about the Israelite woman Hannah, who recited the first silent prayer in the biblical record at the tabernacle at Shiloh.

The biblical Hannah's story is a sad one. She was childless and she wanted a child, so she came to the tabernacle entrance and just went ahead and poured out her soul directly to God. Every successor to Hannah who prays to God in a synagogue, Temple, or anywhere, engages in an analogous mystical act and shares in the belief that his or her words or thoughts somehow unacoustically travel to God's ear.

Here is Hannah's short narrative:

Once, when they had finished eating and drinking in Shiloh, Hannah stood up. Now Eli the priest was sitting on a chair by the doorpost of the Lord's temple.

In bitterness of soul Hannah wept much and prayed to the Lord. ...

As she continued praying before the Lord, the priest Eli observed her mouth. Hannah was speaking in her heart; only her lips moved, and her voice was not heard. Therefore Eli took her to be a drunken woman.

Eli (to Hannah): How long will you go on being drunk? Put your wine away.

Hannah: No, my lord, I am a woman troubled in spirit. I have drunk neither wine nor strong drink, but I have been pouring out my soul before the Lord. Do not regard your servant as a worthless woman, for all along I have been speaking out of my great anxiety and vexation.

Eli: Go in peace, and may the God of Israel grant your petition that you have made to him.

Hannah: Let your servant find favor in your eyes.

Then the woman went her way and ate, and her face was no longer sad.

Eli the priest could not understand that Hannah, or any sober person, could think that they could speak directly yet silently to God. The priest believed that only he and his brethren controlled the access to the sacred. All requests had to be vocalized and ritualized, and had to go through him, according to his ways and the directions of the holy place. Eli acted as if he was the gatekeeper of heaven, as he is depicted in the story, sitting on a chair at the entrance to the Temple. As told, once Hannah explains her acts, Eli accepts her sincerity and intercedes for Hannah. He assures her that God will grant her non-vocal request.

Eli had for Hannah, in this anecdote, just one accusatory and rhetorical question. I have more to ask Hannah about what she thought that she was doing there at the sacred place of Israelite worship. Here are some of the things that I want to know:

> Hannah, what was your imagined experience while standing at the holy site and reciting your prayers?
>
> When pouring out your soul, did you feel transported to heavenly realms to be with the angels, closer to God?
>
> Did you seek to relive the experiences of salvation, along with the Israelites, as they miraculously walked through the dry land of the split sea on their way out of slavery in Egypt?
>
> Did you want to sense the excitement of the anticipation of the redemption of Israel at the end of days and to hear the footsteps of the coming of the messiah?

As these questions suggest, along the spectrum, I want to explore and better understand the mystical, the mythic, and even the kabbalistic varieties of direct religious experiences and their qualities and intensities.

The biblical Hannah appears to me at first to represent a mystic at the most basic, entry level, i.e., one who seeks an encounter with God by talking to him. Everyone praying in the synagogue emulates the biblical Hannah the mystic, the founder of all silent personal prayer in Judaism, an archetype of Jewish religious liturgical experience. She explained her actions to Eli the priest at ancient Shiloh. He was satisfied by her explanation and told her that God will grant her request.

More advanced mystics may engage in a fuller experience, with more bells and whistles. They may delve further into the *mythic* life of religion, which I speak about below. And the most advanced mystics may reach out to even more transcendental and esoteric categories of experience, like those associated with the later Kabbalists.

Let's meet Hannah's direct contemporary descendants in our synagogue and ask them to explain to us more about the experiential notions of Judaism that they find there.

Mystical Experience

To inquire further into the spectrum of religious experience in Judaism, let's return now to the Har-El synagogue in Jerusalem, the mystical place I spoke about in my opening chapter above. As you may recall, that small *shul* was where I once found the perfect *davening*.

At Har-El, I meet one woman who prays there regularly, one of the biblical Hannah's contemporary incarnations. She will be my spokesperson for the contemporary "mystical" archetype in the synagogue. I call her Hannah too. I ask her to explain more of what she believes goes on when she prays.

She tells me that there are other domains of meaning in the universe that we can become acquainted with and learn from. We must accept that there are dimensions of reality beyond this physical world that we inhabit.

Our contemporary Hannah assures me that she is a mild and basic sort of mystic. She reminds me that, after all, in spite of her yearnings and proclivities, she still attends the synagogue. She has not left to join a Kabbalah Center or some other center for spiritual practice, somewhat down the road from the synagogue at another location along the spiritual spectrum.

Our Hannah tells me that it is fair to classify her as mystical archetype and that she embraces the major mythic elements of Judaism. But she surely cautions me that I may not call her a Kabbalist.

Hannah advises me that there is no distinctive profession or status for any of the forms of our mystic archetypes. "Mystical" is more of a description of a discrete personality or mindset—a conglomeration of values as they relate to ultimate questions of the regions of heaven and Earth, the dimensions of time, past and future, and the inhabitants of those other domains.

Hannah assures me that, as a mystic archetype, she ordinarily is comfortable with the views and practices of the scribe, an ideal synagogue type whom we will discuss in the next chapter in greater detail. Both of these types find intuitive the notion that the sacred can be made more personal.

By contrast Hannah does not feel as comfortable with the values of the priest—another ideal synagogue type whom we will discuss later in detail. Previously, in looking at the biblical account, we saw that, as a self-declared independent mystic personality, the ancient Hannah acts as if she has her own entrée into a realm of the holy. That challenges the priest's exclusive control over access to the sources of the sacred and it questions the priest's authority over the centralized locus of ritual.

Hannah, our basic contemporary mystical archetype, professes knowledge of a vision of heaven occupied by creatures who are close to God and who recite praises. She relies on the notion that the domains in heaven, which are inhabited by celestial beings, are knowable to ordinary persons like her. Hannah explains to us what happens when she recites the texts associated with those occupants of heaven. It is not as if she comes into the proximity of an immediate experience of the divine power. Hannah holds to a more uncomplicated notion that to know how to pray effectively, to address her prayer to God, she simply must ask the angels how to talk to Him.

In my discussion of the scribe in the next chapter, I will consider a passage that is recited in the morning liturgy before the biblical verses of the Shema. I preview it now because that selection has a vivid example of this basic mystical expression. It speaks of how the mythical heavenly beings offer praise to the Lord:

> Then the Ophanim and the Holy Hayot, with a roar of noise, raise themselves toward the Seraphim and, facing them, give praise, saying: Blessed be the Lord's glory from His place. (Ezekiel 3)
>
> To the blessed God they offer melodies.
> To the King, living and eternal God,
> They say psalms and proclaim praises.

When Hannah, as an entry-level mystic, says this prayer, she is sure that it will be effective on her behalf. And how does she know that? Because Hannah is certain that no being in the universe knows better than the angels what to say when praying to God.

Hannah invites us to look next at another mystical instance of prayer, the Kedushah—the expression par excellence that the creatures of heaven recite in the proximity to God. Here is how it is formulated in the Kedushah and recited at the repetition of the Amidah:

> We will sanctify your name on earth, as they sanctify it in the highest heavens, as it is written by your prophet, "And they [the angels] call to one another saying: 'Holy, holy, holy is the Lord of hosts the whole earth is full of His glory.'" (Isaiah 6)

> Those facing them say "Blessed–" "Blessed is the Lord's glory from his place." (Ezekiel 3)

> And in your Holy Writings it is written thus: "The Lord shall reign forever. He is your God, Zion, from generation to generation, Halleluyah!" (Koren Siddur, p. 112)

What is so special about this prayer of the angels? On the surface level, it is an involution, a prayer to the second power, a prayer about a prayer. It's like a diary entry by a more advanced mystic who has been to heaven and back, and who has reported what she saw there. She tells us then with a certain awe that this is how the angels sing to praise God, and concludes with the glorious, Halleluyah, which actually means no more than "Praise God."

Hannah explains to us what is remarkable about this prayer of the angels embedded inside of a prayer of the mystic. What the angels actually say is unique, mostly in style and hardly at all in substance. The angels know how to articulate the few special mystical terms such as 'holy' and 'glory' and 'blessed.' The special knowledge of the beginning mystic in this case is her insight into the *way* the angels say the praise, more than the extent of *what* the phrases they say actually signify. Perhaps she makes an assumption here that the right words must be said in the right order to maintain some ecstatic vision or connection between the mystic and heaven; the wrong word will end the rapture and dissipate the ecstasy of that union but the suitable phrase will maintain the mystic's relationship with the bliss of heaven, or simply allow her to communicate properly with God.

Hannah invites us to examine next the well-known and practiced Kaddish prayer, a second case of the entry level mystic's prayers. There are several varieties of Kaddish recited in the synagogue, enough to confuse the beginner. One of them, called the Half (*chatzi*) Kaddish, because a few sentences are left off of it, is recited by the leader of the services as a framing mechanism to mark the end of each major section of the liturgy. And, coincidentally, the term 'half' (*chatzi*) relates to the Hebrew word for a dividing or framing action.

The second Kaddish variety, called the complete one (*shalem*), marks the very end of the services proper.

The best-known Kaddish in the synagogue though is the mourner's Kaddish (*yatom*), the one that is employed as a mourner's doxology (i.e., a praise of God). The practice of associating this prayer with a mourner first appears in the thirteenth century. The synagogue authorities endorsed the custom that mourners during the first eleven months after losing a close relative ought to rise and recite a Kaddish on their own. In the case of this Kaddish Yatom, the mourner rises in his place in the synagogue and recites the doxology at a few appointed times in the daily, Sabbath, and festival services.

I ask Hannah, What is it that the prayer tells us? And, in particular, what makes the prayer an apt mystical enactment for the mourner who recites it? She explains that the substance of the prayer is not at all philosophical or deep. It is a litany, as a mystical prayer is wont to be, of the right words of praise of God in the correct order. She shows us the mystical component of the Kaddish, those lines that cite for us the adoration that is recited by the angels in heaven.

Hannah explains then that reciting the Kaddish provides an appropriate vicarious association for the mourner—to stand and recite a prayer on behalf of the departed souls of the dead:

Magnified and sanctified
may his great name be
in the world he created by his will.
May he establish his kingdom
in your lifetime and in your days,
and in the lifetime of all the house of Israel,
swiftly and soon—and say: Amen.
May his great name be blessed forever and all time.
Blessed and praised, glorified and exalted,
raised and honored, uplifted and lauded
be the name of the Holy One, blessed be he,
beyond any blessing, song, praise and consolation
uttered in the world—and say: Amen
May there be great peace from heaven,
and life for us and for all Israel—and say: Amen.
May he who makes peace in his high places,
make peace for us and for all Israel—and say: Amen.
(Koren Siddur, p. 178)

This lilting and poetic passage does have a certain unique cadence, yet it seems to us in its words to be no more than a standard glorification of God, nothing about death or dying or the deceased. I ask again, why then is this prayer especially apropos for a mourner? Hannah proposes that it is because reciting this heavenly angelic Aramaic praise is the epitome of a mystic's liturgy. It is a stand-in enactment by the mourner on behalf of the departed loved one. The mourner stands in place in the synagogue and recites the words.

But acting in the mode of the mystic archetype, the mourner advances to the next level of mystical prayer. She is not just addressing God with the outpourings of her personal anxiety and vexation, but imagining that she is standing aloft in heaven, representing the soul of her beloved departed, knocking on heaven's door to seek entry for that spirit into a secure, eternal place close to the divine light and near the warmth of God.

I pressed Hannah on this matter. I asked her to clarify to us what is going on when she recites the Kaddish. Is she addressing God from her pew, using the words authorized by the angels on behalf of the deceased? Or is she imagining her ascent to heaven to plead there for the soul of the departed?

Hannah did not know the origins of the Kaddish as a mystic's prayer on behalf of the soul. Alan Mintz explained that this association began in the Middle Ages (*Hurban: Responses to Catastrophe in Hebrew Literature*, pp. 100-101):

> In the generations immediately following the First Crusade the ceremony of remembering the dead began to be practiced not only in the case of renowned rabbinical martyrs of public persecution but also simply for all who died natural deaths, entirely irrespective of the conditions of persecution. A bereaved son would recite the Kaddish, an Aramaic doxology, for the memory of his recently departed father or mother, in the conviction that such recitation had the power to save the deceased's soul from tortures beyond the grave. The practice gained headway in the thirteenth century and by the fifteenth a new custom emerged: the Yorzeit, the recitation of the Kaddish on the anniversary of the death of a relative. And soon there was further established the Yizkor or Hazkarat Neshamot, the Kaddish together with various supplications for the souls of the departed, recited on the Day of Atonement and the last days of the Pilgrimage Festivals. Taken together, this amounts of a kind of cult of the dead that began in medieval Ashkenaz and later spread to all of world Jewry.

Mintz commented further about the deep personal attachment that Jews have to this prayer:

> The astounding tenacity of this outlook is observable in the simple sociological fact, known to all, that in the process of secularization, and especially in the acculturation of Jewish immigrants from Eastern Europe to America, the recitation of the mourner's Kaddish with its attendant rites is the very last particle of tradition to be given up.

Without knowing anything about the historical development of the Kaddish, the entry-level mystic in the synagogue does engage in some prayer, emulating the angels and sending praises and petitions heavenward. She also may practice an intermediate form of mystical prayer, an imagined ascent to stand in another realm and importune her case before the angels and before God.

Judaism also does know about more advanced or full-scale mystical pursuits. In such, the practitioner learns more of the mystical codes, secrets, symbols and signs and seeks a longer and fuller mystical practice and even more vivid experiences of heavenly ascent. It happens that, over the centuries, advanced mystics did not become dominant and persistent presences in the synagogue. They mainly practiced apart, leaving the domain of the synagogue to the entry-level mystics, along with the other common archetypes that we meet and describe in this book, in our model congregation of the faithful.

I might treat those advanced mystics in another book, which I could call, *The People You Meet at a Kabbalah Center*. I do imagine you'd meet there numerous more extensive mystics, and also a fair number of mystically adept meditators, celebrity-monotheists and performers—our artist-poet-musicians. I do not expect you would find there that many scribes or priests. But the details of all that speculation will have to await an account in a future book about a separate visit to an altogether different Jewish religious venue.

Mythical Discourse

Hannah left me with this thought, reminding me that only one letter changes the "mystical" into the "mythical." I ought to spend some time investigating the role of the mythical in the synagogue, she suggested. Maybe I will find another identifiable archetype, like Moshe the Mythic.

Hannah is quite right that I need to explore myTHical synagogue discourse, that mode of thinking, which is indeed related to—but not identical with—the mySTical.

I don't, however, endorse Hannah's suggestion that the mythical element in the synagogue is archetypal. I see that the mythical is a pervasive underlying mode of thought that religious Jews who attend the synagogue accept as a given. You may rightly ask, if it is such a given, then please explain already what you mean by the mythical.

I employ the term "myth" in a manner that is common in the academic study of religions, not in the way it is used in popular culture. In the latter, a myth is a fantasy, a far-fetched untruth that other people wish you to believe, often so they can deceive you or, perhaps, entertain you. By contrast, in the disciplines of the study of religions, a myth denotes a narrative that is truer than true, a story whose details are not just interesting, dramatic or entertaining. The elements of a mythic narrative bear special deep and timeless meanings for those who retell them.

In the prayers that I've considered, I've provided examples of mythic thinking and speaking. My descriptions of the *mystical* in the section just above in this chapter is based on a cosmic *mythical* understanding of the universe. The shared narrative, to which we made reference, presumes that heaven exists, that angels dwell there and that God also does. Those are essential components of a Judaic cosmic myth based on biblical and rabbinic teachings.

More familiar to most of us are the historical myths, the familiar biblical narratives revered in Judaism, such as the exodus of the Israelites from Egypt and the miracle of the splitting of the Red Sea, the revelation of the Torah by God to Moses at Mount Sinai, the wanderings of the Israelites in the desert, the conquest of the Promised Land by Joshua, the construction of the Temple in Jerusalem, the destruction of the Temple and the exile from the land.

Again, by calling them myths, I mean that these are accounts of events that I deem to be more than historical, true or factual. They contain spiritual meanings of great consequence.

As we saw in the previous section, these myths can be *referenced* and they can be *relived*. For instance, the mystic *refers* to the cosmic myths of heaven and angels so she can learn how to pray. The mystic *relives* the myths of heaven and of the angels and (in one way that we interpreted the Kaddish) she sees herself rise to stand in heaven and, there, to beseech God for entry for the soul of the deceased.

In Judaism, historical myths are referenced and relived frequently in the synagogue and in the rituals of the Jewish home. In the synagogue at the end of the morning Shema service, the *berakhot* that are recited right before the Amidah make reference to the song that the Israelites sang after they were brought forth from slavery and saved from the Egyptians by the miracle of the splitting of the sea.

That is a perfect example of how, by making reference to the mythical narratives of Judaism, the people in the synagogue find the right words to praise God. It is as if in the prayer that I cite now, the archetypes of the synagogue turn to and ask an Israelite who has been freed from bondage and who has crossed the Red Sea on dry land, "What should I say to thank God for his saving graces?"

> You have always been the help of our ancestors, Shield and Savior of their children after them in every generation. Your dwelling is in the heights of the universe, and your judgments and righteousness reach to the ends of the earth. Happy is the one who obeys your commandments and takes to heart your teaching and your Word. You are the Master of your people and a mighty King who pleads their cause. You are the first and you are the last. Beside you, we have no king, redeemer or savior. From Egypt you redeemed us, Lord our God, and from the slave-house you delivered us. All their firstborn you killed, but your firstborn you redeemed. You split the Sea of Reeds and drowned the arrogant. You brought your beloved ones across. The water covered their foes; not one of them was left.
>
> For this, the beloved ones praised and exalted God, the cherished ones sang psalms, songs and praises, blessings and thanksgivings to the King, the living and enduring God. High and exalted, great and awesome, he humbles the haughty and raises the lowly, freeing captives and redeeming those in need, helping the poor and answering his people when they cry out to him.
>
> (Stand in preparation for the Amidah. Take three steps back before beginning the Amidah.)
>
> Praises to God Most High, the Blessed One who is blessed. Moses and the children of Israel recited to you a song with great joy, and they all exclaimed: "Who is like you, Lord, among the mighty? (Exodus 15) Who is like you, majestic in holiness, awesome in praises, doing wonders?" With a new song, the redeemed people praised your name at the seashore. Together they all gave thanks, proclaimed your

kingship, and declared: "The Lord shall reign forever and ever (Exodus 15)."

Rock of Israel! Arise to the help of Israel. Deliver, as you promised, Judah and Israel. Our Redeemer, the Lord of hosts is his name, the Holy One of Israel (Isaiah 47). Blessed are you, Lord, who redeemed Israel. (Koren Siddur, pp. 104-106)

These prayers convey to me some important insights, which they derive via a mythical mode of expression. As I suggested, if you want to know how to pray properly, sure, you can ask the angels. But, also, you can recall the mythic redemptions of the history of Israel. The Israelites who crossed the sea on dry land understood firsthand the greatness of God. Therefore, we also may learn from them the best way to pray, and we may follow their lead.

The two conceptual modes of religious thinking that I treat here are related. The mythical is most often a horizontal means of imagining backwards and forwards in history. The mystical, by contrast, is usually a form of vertical visualization upwards to another dimension, towards the heavens.

Both modes have their entry level and their advanced forms of application. As is the case for the mystical, for the mythical there is yet a more advanced form of imagining and reenacting. For example, the Exodus from Egypt is relived in the Seder ritual in the Jewish home ceremonies at the Passover meal. The Haggadah could not make it clearer that a goal of the evening is for the participants to relive the redemption from slavery: "In every generation, a person is obligated to regard herself as if she personally left Egypt." The text spells out the religious obligation for every Jew to relive the miracle of redemption:

We were slaves to Pharaoh in Egypt, and the Lord, our God, took us out from there with a strong hand and with an outstretched arm. If the Holy One, blessed be he, had not taken our ancestors out of Egypt, then we, our children, and our children's children would have remained enslaved to Pharaoh in Egypt. Even if all of us were wise, all of us understanding, all of us knowing the Torah, we would still be obligated to discuss the exodus from Egypt; and everyone who discusses the exodus from Egypt at length is praiseworthy.

The mythical mode of expression is commonly used by all the archetypes we meet in the synagogue. Each of them shows us how to reference and relive their narratives in the different ways that make the most meaningful sense to them.

The Mythic Priest

Just above, we saw how the mystic vividly employs and deploys her mythic narratives of heaven.

Priests, whom we meet formally as synagogue archetypes a bit down the road in our journey (in the chapter "The Priest's Prayers"), get in on a mythic mode of their own by imagining the sacrificial orders of the ancient Temple, by making reference to them and by reliving them. For instance, on the Sabbath, the day of rest, the priest recites at the center of his Amidah prayer, not a long paean to the creation in six days and rest on the seventh, but strikingly something else. He chants a recollection of the sacrifices of the Sabbath day in the ancient Temple.

> You did institute the Sabbath, and did accept its offerings; you did command its special obligations with the order of its drink offerings. They that find delight in it shall inherit glory for everlasting; they that taste it are worthy of life; while those who love its teachings have chosen true greatness. Already from Sinai they were commanded concerning it; and you have also commanded us, O Lord our God, to bring thereon the additional offering of the Sabbath as is proper. May it be thy will, O Lord our God and God of our fathers, to lead us up in joy to our land, and to plant us within our borders, where we will prepare unto you the offerings that are obligatory for us, the continual offerings according to their order, and the additional offerings according to their enactment; and the additional offering of this Sabbath day we will prepare and offer up unto you in love, according to the precept of thy will, as you have prescribed for us in thy Law through the hand of Moses thy servant, by the mouth of thy glory, as it is said:
>
> "And on the Sabbath day two he-lambs of the first year, without blemish, and two tenth parts of an ephah of fine

flour for a meal offering, mingled with oil, and the drink offering thereof: this is the burnt offering of every Sabbath, beside the continual burnt offering and the drink offering thereof." (Numbers 28)

They that keep the Sabbath and call it a delight shall rejoice in thy kingdom; the people that hallow the seventh day, even all of them shall be satiated and delighted with thy goodness, seeing that you did find pleasure in the seventh day and did hallow it; you did call it the desirable of days, in remembrance of the creation.

Our God and God of our fathers, accept our rest; sanctify us by your commandments, and grant our portion in your Law; satisfy us with your goodness, and gladden us with your salvation; purify our hearts to serve you in truth; and in your love and favor, O Lord our God, let us inherit your holy Sabbath; and may Israel, who hallow your name, rest thereon. Blessed are you, O Lord, who hallows the Sabbath.

For the priest, there is no better way to single out what makes the Sabbath special than to reference and relive the service for the day as it was performed on the altar in the ancient Temple in Jerusalem.

And, to further illustrate this point, on the day of great introspection and confession when Jews gather to seek atonement for their sins, in the service for Yom Kippur, the priest invites you to relive the olden activities in the Jerusalem Temple when the High Priest obtained forgiveness for all of the sins of the people of Israel.

The highlight of this ancient service is called the Seder Ha-Avodah (the sacrificial service) in the Musaf Additional Service for Yom Kippur. It describes how the high priest entered into the Holy of Holies, the innermost holy sanctuary of the Temple. He offered there incense and sprinkled blood and then emerged intact from the presence of God and declared God's acceptance of the people of Israel's prayers for atonement.

This lovely, almost childlike narrative of the high priest, tells me the simple things that he did, what he wore, and how his face looked when he finished the ceremony. It stands out as a uniquely vivid mythic story made into a prayer for the Yom Kippur service in the synagogue.

Here is the core of the text of the High Priest's Yom Kippur sacrificial service:

> For his sake you made the covenant of the rainbow as a statute, and in your loving regard of his savory offering, you blessed his children.
>
> You gave him twelve tribes, beloved of the exalted God; they were called "loved ones" from their very birth.
>
> A forehead-plate, a robe, a breastplate, an ephod, a tunic, linen breeches, a turban and a sash.
>
> He was then given the golden vestments which he put on; he sanctified his hands and feet from a golden pitcher.
>
> Arousing within himself feelings of reverence, he entered the Holy of Holies, and when he reached the Ark, he set down the fire-pan between the staves of the Ark.
>
> He transferred all the incense from the ladle into his hands, put it on the glowing coals to the west side and waited there until the Holy of Holies became filled with smoke.
>
> He hastened and took the blood of the bullock from the stand whereon he had placed it, dipped his finger in the blood... and sprinkled from it upon the curtain...
>
> And thus he would count: One!
>
> One and one; one and two; one and three;
>
> one and four; one and five; one and six; one and seven!
>
> When the priests and the people standing in the Temple court heard God's glorious and revered Name clearly expressed by the high priest with holiness and purity, they fell on their knees, prostrated themselves and worshiped; they fell upon their faces and responded: Blessed be the name of his glorious majesty forever and ever.
>
> ...and he took off the golden vestments. His own garments were brought to him and he put them on; and they accompanied him to his house. He would celebrate a festive day for his coming out from the Holy of Holies in peace.
>
> How glorious indeed was the high priest when he safely left the holy of holies!
>
> Like the clearest canopy of heaven was the countenance of the priest.
>
> Like lightning flashing from benign angels was the countenance of the priest.
>
> Like the purest blue of the four fringes was the countenance of the priest.

Like the wondrous rainbow of the bright cloud was the countenance of the priest.

Like the splendor God gave the first creatures was the countenance of the priest.

Like the rose in a beautiful garden was the countenance of the priest.

As I go forward now to the next chapters, I observe that the other ideal synagogue people whom I meet invoke the mythic narratives of Israel for their own purposes. Scribes whom I visit in the next chapter recall the narratives of the sins and punishments of Israel from the book of Deuteronomy to instruct us to keep track of our credits and debits and to fulfill more commandments of the Torah.

Meditators, whom I seek out later on, recall chapters from the past narratives of Israel so as to help them bring compassion and loving kindness to the present experiences of their lives.

To summarize, as I have met the ideal people of my prayers, I have come to realize how the mythic mode looks back in time. It helps bring the narratives of Israel's past to life in the synagogue so that we may find more perfect ways to pray. And, in particular, I've observed how Hannah, our mystic archetype, looks heavenward to learn to pray and even to dare to imagine that, while praying, she transcends her time and place.

In the next four stations of our spiritual journey, we meet four more archetypes of the synagogue: first the scribe, then the priest, the meditator and the celebrity-monotheist. We shall see that they apply the mythic mode of expression with greatly diverse results. They, too, seek to transform their synagogue environs and seek spirituality according to their own understandings of God and Judaism. And, in their worship, they offer up some additional instances of God's favorite prayers.

The Scribe's Prayers

SHEMA

— *n*

1. the central statement of Jewish belief, the sentence "Hear, O Israel: the Lord is your God; the Lord is One" (Deuteronomy 6:4)

2. the section of the liturgy consisting of this and related biblical passages, Deuteronomy 6:4-9 and 11:13-21 and Numbers 15:37-41, recited in the morning and evening prayers and on retiring at night

[Hebrew, literally: hear]

—Collins English Dictionary, 2009

I had the privilege of studying in Rav Aharon Lichtenstein's Talmud *shiur* (class) for two years, 1966-1968. Each December, he invited us *talmidim* (disciples) to his house for latkes (potato pancakes) on Hanukkah. There, in his apartment, we sat with his little kids and his wife Tovah, daughter of Rav Joseph B. Soloveitchik. The latkes were good and the Lichtensteins appeared to be a regular family. For some reason, that surprised me.

Once, during the years that I was in his *shiur*, while I was out with some of the guys playing basketball on the courts between the Yeshiva College dorms, Rav Aharon, a lanky, thin and tall man, came walking by. One of us had the chutzpah to ask him to join the ball game. He said okay and he played aggressively—and just like a regular guy. For some reason, that blew my mind.

And, one year, in our student play, the Yeshiva College Purim *shpiel*, a satiric revue for the holiday, I played the role of Rav Aharon. In my performance, I hemmed and hawed and exaggerated my rebbe's mannerisms much more than I should have. And there in the audience sat my rebbe, laughing heartily along with us. For some reason, that *really* blew my mind.

These three anecdotes aside, Rav Aharon was not just a regular guy. He also was a special teacher who imbued me with indelible lessons that I have taken with me throughout my life.

Rav Aharon taught me that you could be both a humanist and a Talmudic scholar, a *lamdan*. He clearly loved English literature, which he had studied at Harvard. He often and freely quoted poets John Milton and Edmund Spenser. He happily contrasted the ideas of the enlightenment with those of the Torah. But all the time it was clear to me that literature was his avocation and that learning Torah was his true vocation.

Rav Aharon also taught me that you could critically study and deeply love the lifestyle instructions—called the *hashkafah*—of the Torah. Each week, we read and discussed a chapter in Rabbi Elimelech Bar Shaul's inspirational Hebrew treatise, *Mitzvah Valev* (Tel Aviv, 1956), which means the commandments and the heart. Through that work, Rav Aharon taught us that the cognitive understanding of a commandment needed to be joined to the emotional commitment of one's heart. His lessons had a profoundly powerful and positive impact on my faith.

Finally, Rav Aharon taught me that you could be a vitally creative pedagogue even in the most traditional subjects of learning. The college administration told him that he had to give us exams in Talmud, the main subject that he taught us, so he used that as an opportunity to teach us more. He gave us thought-questions. Based on something we learned previously, he would ask us to resolve a new scenario. Or he would give us text-questions. He would have us examine a brand new text, related to some passage we had learned before, and then he asked us to parse it and to comment on it. We had to decide what commentary he had plucked the text from, tell him what the text meant and then explain why we came to our conclusions. That was hard.

That is how Rav Aharon taught me that an exam could do more than ask a student to regurgitate what he had learned. The rabbi tested my knowledge and my thinking powers at the same time, and was the only teacher that I ever had who truly knew details of my personal styles of learning and of my own intellectual strengths and weaknesses. I happily confess that I used elements of Rav Aharon's methodology of thought-questions and text-questions in many of the Talmud and Jewish Studies courses that I taught over the years at the University of Minnesota, the Jewish Theological Seminary and elsewhere.

After I went on to become a professor, I would take extended leaves to work on my research in Jerusalem, Israel. My father owns a Katamon-neighborhood apartment that he inherited from his parents, who moved to Israel in the 1950s from New York City. That is where I lived while in Jerusalem. In the mornings, I frequently would go to the *shacharit* morning services at the Shtiblach nearby.

The Shtiblach was a veritable prayer mall, a busy set of connected, one-room prayer-halls in a single, modest neighborhood building. There, I would often see the saintly Rav Aharon at one of the services, sitting near him and thereby joining him de facto at prayer. That would lift my spirits for the day.

Because Rav Aharon embodies the ideals of the scribe archetype, I use his name to refer now to that remarkable model of prayer that I met during my spiritual quests in search of perfect prayer.

Instructions

A few instructions for reading this chapter

1. Focus your attention on this book. If you are interrupted while you are reading this paragraph by someone who speaks to you, do not stop to reply, unless the person is your boss or someone of authority or importance in your life. And do not initiate a conversation with anyone while you are concentrating on this part of these instructions.

2. Only after you finish reading the first paragraph of these instructions, may you stop and initiate an important conversation, or may you reply to anyone who wishes to speak with you.

Really, now? Do I need instructions for when to talk and when to be silent while I am reading this book?

That's pretty much what puzzled me when I first read the rabbinic instructions in the law code, the Mishnah, (published around 200 CE) about how to recite the short daily prayer of three paragraphs, called the Shema. The rabbis prescribe there how to act while you read the prayer. And they debated the finer nuances of how one must focus and when one may talk while engaged in the recitation:

> "At the breaks [between the paragraphs of the Shema] one may extend a greeting [to his associate] out of respect, and respond [to a greeting which was extended to him]."

> "And in the middle [of reciting a paragraph] one may extend a greeting out of fear [of a person] and respond," the words of R. Meir.

> R. Judah says, "In the middle [of reciting a paragraph] one may extend a greeting out of fear and respond out of respect.

> "At the breaks [between reciting the paragraphs] one may greet out of respect and respond to the greetings of any man." (Mishnah Berakhot 2:1)

For some time after I first studied this bit of Talmudic law, I was satisfied to explain that this is the rabbis' way of discussing part of a religious ritual that they called *kavvanah*—focus. I concluded that this is how the ancients talked about the focus and concentration we need to attain so as to add solemnity to a prayer ritual.

But it nagged at me. Why speak about greetings when you are talking about focus? What more were they telling me by framing the rules as they did?

Then, some time later, while working one day at my computer, writing about Jewish prayer, my wife came in to tell me that she was going out to appointments and wanted me to know her plans for the day.

"Just a minute," I said. "I do want to hear what you are saying. Please just let me concentrate to finish writing this paragraph..."

Aha. I understood a lot at the moment that I said that. It became clear to me that, when the rabbis spoke about focus— *kavvanah*—for reciting the Shema, they used a model of concentration that was familiar to a writer—to a person who is engaged in textual work, to a scholar sitting at his desk and trying to think through his complete thoughts.

Now that you have met Rav Aharon, you will want to know what else it means when we say that he is a scribe.

Here, then, is how some scribes concentrate. A writer needs to focus on composing a paragraph from the beginning until the end. Similarly, an accountant needs to finish scanning and calculating a column of numbers from top to bottom. A lawyer must complete the reasoning of the steps of an argument all the way through. A programmer must reach the end of writing a complex subroutine of computer code. All of those professions fit into the category of a reflective writing and calculating worker—a scribe.

Formulating matters in this way, I finally understood in greater depth what the rabbis in the Mishnah told me in their rules for focus for reading the Shema in the synagogue.

And my final step of discovery came when I understood that this meant that the Shema was the prayer of a specific archetype, which I call the *scribe*.

The Scribe's Personality

Now that I have introduced you to the scribe, here are some of the things you will want to know about this person. I'll put this before you as a scribe would, in the style of an article about him from a hypothetical *Encyclopedia of Synagogue Archetypes*.

This archetype represents the literate professionals in a community. The scribe may function in a range of settings. He writes, maintains and publishes books and documents. He serves as the record keeper of the society, as a bureaucrat in local administration of the village and in more centralized roles in politics and in the Temple. A scribe may serve in your community as an accountant or a lawyer in a commercial setting—both of those are noted experts in regulations and codes of law.

The scribe in our idealized town writes all of the official documents for businesses and for families. He is immersed in civil and criminal law. He may take to writing a rulebook or a code of practices as a way to express the regulations of life. Certainly, one main essence of the nature of the ancient Talmud—its legal materials—emerged out of the culture of scribes.

I've encountered many references to scribes in my work on ancient Judaism. The scribe of old serves as teacher of sacred and secular wisdom. I take for granted that a large proportion of the ancient rabbis identified strongly with the scribal archetype and personified their ideals. As you would expect, over the centuries, actual specialized Jewish writing professionals called scribes produced popular religious products, namely Torah scrolls, amulets, tefillin, and mezuzot.

Many of us come in contact with scribes in our daily lives. Our relatives and friends who are lawyers, accountants and writers fall squarely within this archetype. Information technology developers, programmers and engineers also fit the category.

The scribe needs to get along with the other people in his community, with the other five vibrant and colorful archetypal people in our timeless synagogue, namely, the priest, meditator, mystic, celebrity and performer (artist-poet-musician).

The scribe relates to those other ideal types in a variety of ways. This archetype maintains one-to-one, open, and intermediary relations with the priests and political leaders, with administrators and merchants, community organizers and householders. However, he is not seen primarily by his community as a prominent public figure nor does he—for the most part—have interest in assuming a leading political role in the community. Scribes do not hold to grand or national aspirations or visions, except as they bestow meaning on the day-to-day life of the village.

Our scribe archetype overlaps the most in his interests with the meditator, mystic and performer (artist–poet–musician) archetypes.

Using meditative acts to express religion appeals to him. He finds meaning in blessings—which I will identify in my discussion of "The Meditator's Prayers" in a chapter below as the quintessence of Judaic meditation. Scribes assiduously promulgate their use. The practices of the meditator are a big part of the scribe's daily personal practice—affording him a means to cultivate a distinctive character of life and to lay claim to sanctifying many mundane practices in his daily routines.

That attitude brings the scribe into conflict with some of the priestly purposes for religious practice. As I discuss in my account of the ideal type that I call the priest in the next chapter, they prefer to divert the hoi polloi and chattering masses away from a thoughtful meditative focus on their daily conditions, away from dealing with the here and now. The priest would rather have you turn the center of your religious imagination and attention to both the heavens above and to the messianic time to come.

In my discussion of the priests, I point out that they need to connect to their sacred spaces, to have their Temples. By contrast, my friends the scribes have no vested interest in advancing the influence of the idea of the centralization of divine power or the notion of the inherent holiness of designated spaces—ideas that are so important to the priest figure.

Hence, scribes find attractive the mystic's notion that, through mimicry of the prayers of the angels, Israelites can speak more efficiently and directly to God. And they can do this without any reference to a Temple. That mystic character befits the scribe. It allows him direct access to images of the deity and the realms of heaven above.

Now that you have met the scribe in a more detailed overview and gotten to know a bit about him, let's look at examples of how he prays, how he expresses his needs and addresses God. Let's turn first to the scribe's main prayer, the Shema, and see in particular how he incorporates in it his scribal values together with the imagery of the mystic. As we meet and get to know the six ideal people in the synagogue, we find that they do share elements of style and overlap in the contents of their respective prayers. This is one such example.

The blessing *Yozer Or* that frames and introduces the morning Shema instructs us regarding the ways the beings of heaven praise God:

> All accept on themselves,
> One from another, the yoke of the kingdom of heaven,
> Granting permission to one another
> To sanctify the One who formed them,
> In serene spirit,
> Pure speech and sweet melody.
> All, as one,
> Proclaim his holiness, saying in awe:
> "Holy, holy, holy is the Lord of hosts:
> the whole world is filled with his glory." (Isaiah 6)
> Then the Ophanim and the Holy Hayot,
> with a roar of noise,
> raise themselves toward the Seraphim and,
> facing them, give praise, saying:
> "Blessed be the Lord's glory from his place." (Ezekiel 3)
> To the blessed God they offer melodies.
> To the King, living and eternal God,
> They say psalms and proclaim praises. (Koren Siddur, p. 94)

Why, I ponder, does the scribe invoke the angelic model for praying in this melodic prayer? Who knows better, he says, how to address the deity than those closest to God? The scribe knows that, when you want to get something done right, go to the specialist. So we go to the angels and they tell us how we can best formulate our prayers.

The sharing of content, themes and expressions among our synagogue archetypes is common. Of course, the priest knows as well to model prayers after those of the angelic heavenly experts. He does something similar in the Kedushah in the Amidah, making references of his own to the angels. But, in that instance, as I will point out in my discussion of the priest's prayers in the next chapter, what he does seems to me to be imitative and derivative rather than integral to his liturgical voice.

I feel the same about the derivative way that the priest uses the blessing formula. We'll see that the priest formulates his major prayer as a set of compact blessings, epitomized in the nineteen that are found in the Amidah. Those blessings don't appear to me to achieve the meditative purposes that the scribe realizes through his own more elaborate blessings and prayers, again as I explain more fully in the section on the priest's prayers.

I get the sense that the scribes agree with enthusiasm with the values of the mystic and the meditator. Priests seem to me to adopt halfheartedly the values of those archetypes.

Surely, these two archetypes—scribes and priests—now that they are praying together in the same synagogues, are good friends. But, in the prayer services, even after all the efforts by editors and liturgists to meld together the prayer book, the seams among the archetypes and their expressions still remain obvious to me.

One small but provocative example jumped out at me after I started to look for these two distinct personalities in the prayers. In his major prayer, the Amidah, the priest actually gently denigrates the scribe. The prayer asks God to have compassion for "the remnant of their scribes" along with the "righteous converts" and "upon us."

> Upon the righteous, upon the pious, upon the elders of your people, the House of Israel, upon the remnant of their scribes, upon the righteous converts and upon us, may your compassion be aroused, Lord our God.
>
> Grant ample reward to all who sincerely trust in your Name, and place our lot with them so that we may never be ashamed, for we have put our trust in you. Blessed are you, Lord, who is the support and the trust of the righteous.

Putting aside the hints of competition or of conflicting views among the scribe and the other archetypes, what can I say further now about the core views, values and relationships of my friend, the scribe?

Scribes, who in general derive their main influence and power from access to detailed knowledge of laws, records and stories, particularly esteem and cherish the contents of the Torah and delight in enumerating its commandments.

The scribes whom I know are the kinds of people who seek after social stability and stasis, since both are necessary for the performance of their trades. For these reasons, it's logical that scribes are at odds with some of the values of political figures who seek to foster ferment or change. They also likely prefer to stifle socially unsettling religious types such as faith healers or magical thinkers. Scribes should be working hard to render mute those disruptive voices and keep them out of the synagogue.

Our friends the priests take a broader—even universal— view of their roles in the world. Even though the scribes have minimal interest in politics outside of the immediate learning circles of their villages, they may be the ones who keep the annals and write the technical manuals for the technology of the Temple's network connections to the sacred. The scribe serves the politicians or priests as an employee or writer. He works for them, but that does not mean he identifies with their core global values.

In accord with his own value system, in short, the scribe identifies God's revelation closely with a set of texts, the canonical texts of Judaism.

Let's look at another prayer that I classify as scribal to see how it expresses these values most clearly. The *Ahavah Rabbah* blessing, which frames the morning Shema, invokes the themes of the love God and the reverence for Torah, along with the idea of salvation:

> Instill in our hearts the desire to understand and discern, to listen, learn and teach, to observe, perform and fulfill all the teachings of your Torah in love. Enlighten our eyes in your Torah and let our hearts cling to your commandments. Unite our hearts to love and revere your name, so that we may never be ashamed. And because we have trusted in your holy, great and revered name, may we be glad and rejoice in your salvation. (Koren Siddur, p. 96)

The scribe's notion of what is holy, as I said, is not dependent on knowing God's address, on identifying and managing his sacred spaces or precincts. To serve God, you must love him, know how to fill God's needs, wear the clothes he wants you to wear—e.g., phylacteries on your head and fringes on your garments—and prepare and eat the foods he wants you to eat.

And let us not forget that, in the synagogue when we meet the scribe, we see him sitting while reciting his Shema, in the posture that is deemed proper, practical and most common for scribes at their work.

A Scribe's Aria

The Passover Seder is one of the great operas of Jewish liturgy. In the numerous acts and scenes of this home production, several of the archetypes of Jewish prayer take the stage to perform. The meditator, the scribe and the performer take their turns. The celebrity and mystic make brief appearances. And the priest remains mostly offstage in the wings.

I see evidence that the central *Maggid* narrative section of the Seder is mainly a scribal presentation.

The Israelites' liberation from Egypt, the familiar notion of a freed slave, is a prominent theme that I associate with the scribe. In the biblical narrative, which, in fact, underpins all Judaic worldviews, the Israelite servant or slave who was set free becomes the pioneer, the seeker, a wanderer, vagabond or nomad.

In the Passover Seder *Maggid,* the imaginary pilgrim reenacts the journey of the pioneer, while all the time remaining at the Passover table engaged in the lengthy study of a Midrash. The core of this Seder section takes the four verses in Deuteronomy (26:5-8) called the pilgrim's confession—one at a time—and attaches to them rabbinic interpretations.

> And you shall speak and say before the Lord thy God: "A wandering Aramean was my father, and he went down into Egypt, and sojourned there, few in number; and he became there a nation, great, mighty, and populous. And the Egyptians dealt ill with us, and afflicted us, and laid upon us hard bondage. And we cried unto the Lord, the God of our fathers, and the Lord heard our voice, and saw our affliction, and our toil, and our oppression. And the Lord brought us forth out of Egypt with a strong hand and an outstretched arm, and with great terribleness, and with signs, and with wonders."

The Haggadah explores the meaning of those verses, and embellishes the story. This recitation is plainly an occasion of scribal learning. The *Maggid* section of the Haggadah that follows and seeks to answer the four questions is an evening of rabbinic Torah study using the methods of the ancient Midrash.

The Seder looks pretty much like an instance of scribal worship and practice, and not one to associate with any of my other archetypal models.

Its ritual content is not at all priestly—it does not mention the Temple, Jerusalem, genealogy or any other prominent priestly value. It is not mystical—with the exception of the imagined visit of the prophet Elijah that is said to coincide with the recitation of "Pour out thy wrath" upon the nations of the earth. It is not overwhelmingly mythic—no complete narratives of the Exodus or of any other type appear, with the exception of the mythic requirement that everyone at the Seder must imagine himself as if he went forth from Egypt. It is not kabbalistic—no heavenly creatures are invoked, with the exception of the angel who visited death upon the Egyptian first-born. It is not meditative, no element of compassion is invoked and few original meditative blessings for this event are recited. And it is not celebratory—with the exception of the single paragraph that I mentioned, "Pour out thy wrath." It is a great instance of performance, but not a straight reading of biblical passages. By the elimination of our other archetypes, this then must be a scribal affair.

Before the meal is served on the Passover evening, all of the talk in the Haggadah that we are familiar with at the Seder ends. Only then do we find the one solitary recollection of the Temple. The leader speaks about the bones of the paschal offering—the shank bone that is on the Seder plate. The householder lifts up the bone and recollects, "Why do we have this Passover bone in front of us tonight?" He answers that it is because the angel of death passed over the houses of the Israelites in Egypt when he went on to slay the first-born of the Egyptians.

That historical reference to Egypt and the lifting of the bone are all that we manage to mention and do at the Seder to recall the Passover sacrifice. We make no recollection in the core of the service of the great throngs of Israelites that gathered together in Jerusalem at the Temple each year to bring their Passover offering. We say nothing at all about the priests or the sanctuary.

By omission, this seems to us to be a denigration of the priests by the scribes, a way of reminding the priests of their bygone past glory in a Temple that no longer stands.

The Scribe's Values

Now that you have met him and examined some of his prayers, you ask, can I summarize then—what does the scribe believe? Let me review the essence of the scribe's formative religious principles.

The scribes value the written word, record keeping, books and learning, social stability. Symbolically this takes expression in valuing Torah and mitzvot above other Judaic values. They like the visions of religious practices in the book of Deuteronomy and in particular they prefer the conceptions of God expressed there.

Now let's turn our focus to the most prominent liturgical case in point for the scribe—the biblical passages that constitute the Shema and its accompanying blessings.

The sermons in the book of Deuteronomy—in the biblical texts that constitute the core of the Shema—resonate for the scribes.

Just what does that mean? It means first that they accept and understand that there is a God who keeps records and pays out on accounts, according to what was paid in. Those scribal values are essential to the Shema liturgy—the first of its two biblical passages, Deuteronomy 6, comes right out with a theological agenda with which the scribes identify (6-9). They call this the statement in which they agree to, "the acceptance of the dominion of heaven."

> And these words that I command you today shall be on your heart. You shall teach them diligently to your children, and shall talk of them when you sit in your house, and when you walk by the way, and when you lie down, and when you rise. You shall bind them as a sign on your hand, and they

shall be as frontlets between your eyes. You shall write them on the doorposts of your house and on your gates.

The rabbis later label the second biblical paragraph of the Shema, Deuteronomy 11, with the title, "the acceptance of the yoke of the commandments." That paragraph includes these familiar verses (13-15):

> And if you will obey my commandments which I command you this day, to love the Lord your God, and to serve him with all your heart and with all your soul, he will give the rain for your land in its season, the early rain and the later rain, that you may gather in your grain and your wine and your oil. And he will give grass in your fields for your cattle, and you shall eat and be full.

Scribes subscribe to the basic tenet of the Deuteronomist's theology. You obey God—and he gives you the rain, the rewards for your obedience.

The Scribe's Judgments

This pristine and simple conceptual framework of the scribe archetype's vision of God is reiterated in the synagogue liturgy as one of the loud voices in a popular and dramatic Rosh Hashanah prayer. The medieval *piyyut* (i.e., liturgical poem), *Unetanneh Tokef* tells the vivid story of God's role in the judgment of the High Holidays. As the prayer describes in a boldly scribal idiom, the Shepherd, God, keeps his records in an annual record book and accounts for all of his flock so he can determine the fate of every individual for the coming year.

Let us look at the images in this brief prayer and savor their intricacy. It begins with an invocation of the awe of the day and the kingship of God. That is an overarching theme of the holiday of Rosh Hashanah that can be taken up by several of our archetypes and made part of their expression. The picture of God-as-King has drama for the performer; it can be set in heaven for the mystic; it can be the source of all authority for the scribe; it can be a rallying cry for the celebrity.

> We shall ascribe holiness to this day.
> For it is awesome and terrible.

Your kingship is exalted upon it.
Your throne is established in mercy.
You are enthroned upon it in truth.

The second stanza announces an overt scribal theme, a major direction of this liturgy—that God is not just King but the Great Judge who keeps all of the records in a book:

In truth you are the judge,
The exhorter, the knowing, the witness,
He who inscribes and seals,
who counts and measures.

You remember all that is forgotten.
     You open the book of remembrance
And it announces by itself,
And the seal of each person is there.

The drama unfolds in heaven and the mystic takes control of the prayer in the verses that follow, describing the judgment of the angels in heaven:

The great shofar is sounded,
A still small voice is heard.
The angels are dismayed,
They are seized by fear and trembling
As they proclaim: Behold the Day of Judgment!
     For all the hosts of heaven are brought for judgment.
They shall not be guiltless in your eyes.
And all creatures shall parade before you as a troop.

"As a troop," in the Hebrew, is *bnai maron*. The phrase has several possible derivations and meanings. One of them traces the term back to a Latin word—*numerus*, meaning troop, i.e., soldiers that are counted. Rabbi Judah in the Talmud (Bavli Rosh Hashanah 18a) says it refers to the troops of the House of David. That import coincides with the preceding image of the hosts of heaven passing in judgment before God.

The other meaning sees the term as derived from the Aramaic *emer*, i.e., a sheep. In that case, I would translate the phrase, "All humankind will pass before you like members of a flock," and that would conform well with the image that follows of the shepherd counting and determining which of his sheep will go to slaughter. In the Talmud, an anonymous opinion favors that meaning.

This notion of passing in judgment on Rosh Hashanah comes out of the Mishnah Rosh Hashanah 1:2, which says without much elaboration, "On Rosh Hashanah all who walk the earth pass before Him like *bnai maron*." The Mishnah cites as its basis for this idea Psalms 33:15, "He fashions the hearts of them all and knows all of their deeds." It is a far stretch from the general terms of the verse in Psalms to the particular story for Rosh Hashanah.

Both of the alternatives for translating this High Holiday prayer bear "correct" meanings. The power of this great poetry is its ability to move and transition from one vivid image to another.

Above this poetic line, we ought to visualize that *we* are in the heavenly court where God judges his angels. Below this line, we imagine that we descend to the earthly stockyard where the shepherd separates his sheep. The human, reciting the prayer, stands in between those two realms.

In the mystic's sense, each person sees himself as an eternal creature, a little lower than the angels. And in the scribe's sense, every individual knows that his mortal days are numbered and his life is just as vulnerable as that of a farm animal. The liturgy continues:

> As a shepherd herds his flock,
> Causing his sheep to pass beneath his staff,
> So do you cause to pass, count, and record,
> Visiting the souls of all living,
> Decreeing the length of their days,
> Inscribing their judgment.
> On Rosh Hashanah it is inscribed,
> And on Yom Kippur it is sealed.

The scribe-accountant makes his columns, and they are the format for the next part of his liturgy—a list:

> How many shall pass away and how many shall be born,
> Who shall live and who shall die,
> Who shall reach the end of his days and who shall not,
> Who shall perish by water and who by fire,
> Who by sword and who by wild beast,

Who by famine and who by thirst,
Who by earthquake and who by plague,
Who by strangulation and who by stoning,
Who shall have rest and who shall wander,
Who shall be at peace and who shall be pursued,
Who shall be at rest and who shall be tormented,
Who shall be exalted and who shall be brought low,
Who shall become rich and who shall be impoverished.

The major movements of the poem are complete and now the scribe-lawyer interjects his final advice. Even after the Judge's verdict is sealed, it may help to ply God with letters of recommendation about the good deeds that the defendant has performed. And, then, after all avenues of appeal have been exhausted, it may be best to fall upon the mercy of the court. That is what the prayer prescribes:

> But repentance, prayer and righteousness avert the severe decree.
>
> For your praise is in accordance with your name. You are difficult to anger and easy to appease. For you do not desire the death of the condemned, but that he turn from his path and live. Until the day of his death you wait for him. Should he turn, you will receive him at once. In truth you are their Creator and you understand their inclination, for they are but flesh and blood.

After the scene plays out, the performer takes back the stage to move on from this interlude, with great dramatic flourishes—pure poetry—to the next segment of the service:

> The origin of man is dust, his end is dust. He earns his bread by exertion and is like a broken shard, like dry grass, a withered flower, like a passing shadow and a vanishing cloud, like a breeze that blows away and dust that scatters, like a dream that flies away.
>
> But you are King, God who lives for all eternity! There is no limit to your years, no end to the length of your days, no measure to the hosts of your glory, no understanding the meaning of your Name. Your Name is fitting unto you and you are fitting unto it, and our name has been called by your Name.
>
> Act for the sake of your Name and sanctify your Name through those who sanctify your Name...

(The Kedushah-sanctification prayer follows...)

Indeed the core of this great prayer expresses vivid imagery from the voice of a creative archetypal scribe. It portrays for us a God who sits annually in judgment, reading from a book of records to determine the fate of the Jewish people and of humankind for the coming spiritual year.

In my ideal synagogue, the scribe occupies a prominent place expressing some of the most powerful and evocative ideas of Jewish theology. As I associated these notions with a distinct archetype, I brought them into sharper focus and showed how they contrast and compare with the other threads of personality and perception within the panoply of Jewish worship.

Within this last example of a moving and complex prayer, we watched and listened as the voices of the mystic and scribe competed with each other for our attention, as they spoke to us and as we prayed to God through their personalities in one of God's favorite prayers.

The Priest's Prayers

A·MI·DAH
[ah-**mee**-dah]
—noun Judaism.
a liturgical prayer that is recited in standing position at each of the three daily services and consists of three opening blessings, three closing blessings, and one intermediate blessing on the Sabbath and holy days and 13 intermediate blessings on other days.
Origin: < Heb *ămīdhāh* a standing

—Random House Dictionary, 2010

I learned on my spiritual journey that the priest gets to play two special roles in our synagogue, based not on any talent or merit, but on his lineage alone. First, when we draft synagogue members to ascend to the *bimah* to read the Torah, the priest gets the first call, the honored preference to stand and read from the scroll.

Second, when we say the Musaf Additional Service on the festivals, the priest goes up on the platform in front of the ark of the Torah, turns to face the congregation, raises his hands, and blesses us with the priestly benediction. He solemnly bestows upon us protection, grace and peace with a blessing whose tune is more than two millennia old:

> May the Lord bless you and guard you
> May the Lord make his face shine upon you and be gracious unto you
> May the Lord lift up his face onto you and give you peace
> (Numbers 6)

Sometimes, I try getting an extra blessing from Mr. Cohen, one of the priests in our congregation, when he comes down from the platform. I say to him, "Strength and blessing to you." And he replies to me, by agreed upon social convention, "May you too be blessed."

Why do we consent to have them bless us? Why do we agree to cede to them ritual authority and priority?

It's because these priests comprise our Jewish aristocracy. In ancient Israel, going back millennia in our history, their families served God and represented the people of Israel in the Temple in Jerusalem through their sacrifices and rituals.

Instructions

Instructions for reading this chapter
1. Sit straight up in your chair. Don't slouch. Even better, stand up and hold the book. And be serious.
2. Concentrate intently on this content. If anyone tries to intrude upon your reading, do not stop—not for your boss, not for your wife, not for the phone, not even if the fire alarm goes off in your building. Do not interrupt until you finish reading the whole chapter.

Now, you may say that I am being unreasonable. Who has the capacity for such focus? Where does this idea of intense concentration come from?

I wondered the same thing when I studied the similar rules that the Mishnah prescribes for reciting the Amidah prayer:

> One may stand to pray only with a solemn frame of mind.

> The early pious people tarried a while before they would pray, so that they could direct their hearts to the omnipresent God.

> While one is praying, even if the king greets him, he may not respond.

> Even if a serpent is entwined around his heel, he many not interrupt his prayer. (Mishnah Berakhot 5:1)

For a long time after I first studied this passage, I was satisfied to note that it spoke in rabbinic idiom to prescribe the correct intensity-level of the *kavvanah*—the focus of one's mind—for this prayer. It tells us that, because the Amidah is a more solemn prayer than the Shema, you need to concentrate more intensely when you recite it.

But as you may recall, in the exploration above regarding the scribe, I wondered about the specifications for *kavvanah* for the Shema. I ask again: Why this kind of concentration and not some other? Why these specifications regarding focus for the person who is reciting the Amidah?

The answer came to me one day as I prepared for a lecture that I was to give about the meanings and purposes of the Amidah. I searched around for a picture to put on a PowerPoint presentation, looking for a pose that illustrated the right *kavvanah* for this prayer. I did not want just to insert an image of a man standing in prayer and wrapped around in a *tallit*. That, to me, was a redundant cliché that did not illuminate any meaning.

What, then, would exhibit a person so intent and disciplined that he would not move, no matter how much distraction came into the context of his surroundings? And that is when I realized what this archetype demanded. I typed "palace guard" into Google's image search engine. I found and copied a picture of a stereotypical guard from Buckingham Palace in London, dressed in his red-and-black uniform and standing at attention. I inserted that graphic into my presentation.

I wanted to show the substance of the personality—that, in accord with his archetype, the priest requires a frame of mind of discipline and obedience for the recitation of the Amidah. This means a martial kind of self-possession, standing with erect posture, feet together, facing Jerusalem as specified by the rules for reciting this prayer. The person reciting the prayer needs to bow at the proper intervals, in keeping with his martial drill.

The Mishnah instructs us that not even a coiled serpent at his heel be allowed to distract the *davener* during his recitation of the Amidah prayer; even if a serpent is nearby, he shall not pause his recitation. That means that the priestly-archetype is in authority, in control of his emotions and consciousness—not consequentially ecstatic or meditative in any particular way and, yet, guarded against distraction.

Like the palace guard, the priest archetype who is engaged in prayer is militarily focused on the prescribed activities. He obeys what he is commanded to obey and deliberately ignores all other noises or intrusions into his material context.

Strength and blessing to you, Mr. Cohen. We salute you.

Now that we have saluted our current archetype, the priest, we do need to know some more about his personality. But it is complicated to portray this archetype because there are real people named Mr. Cohen in our brick and mortar synagogues who are certified priests in their lineage, with actual priestly DNA.

Scientists have confirmed that there are identifying markers that define of the lineage of the Israelite priest. Since the year 2000, genetic research has shown scientific evidence that the Jewish priesthood actually existed and continues to exist. The science of this claim is based on examination of a segment of DNA that contains linked gene variations that are inherited together as a unit. Geneticists call that a haplotype.

Michael F. Hammer of the University of Arizona and Karl Skorecki of the Technion—the Israel Institute of Technology—found the DNA marker signature of the Cohanim. They dubbed it Cohen Modal haplotype. Their study from that year traced the patrilineal dynasty of the Jewish priesthood and substantiated the biblical story that Aaron, the brother of Moses, was the first high priest. They profess that their work shows that Aaron was one of a number of common male ancestors in the Cohanim lineage, who lived in ancient Hebrew times, some 3,200 years ago in the Near East.

University of Arizona geneticist Hammer and his colleagues used DNA markers to trace the ancient bloodline to its sources. Their more recent research, in 2009, on the Cohen Y chromosome indicated a refinement in their results. The Jewish priesthood, the Cohanim, was established by several unrelated male lines rather than a single male lineage dating to ancient Hebrew times. This extended their conclusions based on a larger number of markers to provide a better resolution of the history of the Jewish priesthood. Their original model accounts for 30 percent of Cohanim Y chromosomes from both Ashkenazi and non-Ashkenazi Jewish communities and traces it to a common male ancestor that lived some three millennia ago in the Near East. Their newer work adds additional Y chromosome lineages and suggests that the priesthood was established by several unrelated male lines. In 2009, the journal *Human Genetics* published Hammer's newer findings in an article titled, "Extended Y chromosome haplotypes resolve multiple and unique lineages of the Jewish priesthood."

Some of these real people also display the personality traits of archetypal priests—as I define the concept here in our virtual synagogue—and some do not. To put it another way, some have identifiable markers of the *cultural DNA* that I am defining when I delineate our priest archetype and some do not have that cultural DNA.

To explain this better, I discuss some of the information about the historical priests in ancient Israel and I also sketch out, based on the data from the past, the traits of our discovered timeless archetype of the priest.

As I said, the priestly lineage dates back thousands of years in our tradition. The tribes of Israel mostly merged together over the centuries, blurring the tribal distinctions. But the priests retained their familial identities as the descendants of the first priest, Aaron. So, too, did their cousins, the other Levites from the same tribal roots, descended from Levi, the son of Jacob. So, yes, in real synagogues we may sit next to neighbors who identify themselves as priests and Levites, with the physical priest DNA.

These people are the bearers of what little actual aristocracy and special family identifications we Jews have today. In the past, as I noted, their familial status once gave the priests control of a sacred space in Israel. It gave them hegemony over the Temple and all of the cultic acts that were performed within. The priests managed the sacrificial business of the Temple, the offerings of meal and oil, animal sacrifices, purification rites, the calendar, the festivals, and all the appurtenances of those activities. As I see it, any archetypal voice that I label a priest, by definition will value as paramount the sanctity of the ancient Temple and its services.

While priests controlled the Temple in ancient times, they also aligned with the kings of Israel to provide a combination of holy and military leadership for the Israelite state. Most dramatically, King Solomon built a magnificent Jerusalem

Temple, solidifying during that era, in fact and in symbol, the bond between the political and military monarchy and the sacred and tribal priesthood.

Both, then, the historical and the archetypal priests are naturally interested in matters associated with cult, ritual and sacrifice. Growing from this, their concern subsumes the more abstract notions of sin, guilt and atonement, and even the special detailed cases of the spiritual and physical healing of lepers, which fell under the responsibility of the ancient Israelite priests.

To generalize, the priest seeks God through familiar symbols and notions. He longs for and looks for a centralized city and Temple where God abides.

Beyond that, as guardian of the holy Temple precincts and the familial priestly lineage, the priest took strong interest in the genealogy of the tribes—questions of who is a Jew and who is not a Jew, who is a Levite and who is not a Levite. They paid special cognizance to the notion of tribal purity in general, to what evolutionary biologists would call the preservation of the gene.

By virtue of his role as protector of both Temple sanctity and genetic purity, the priest saw the world divided into physical spaces that are either holy, like the Temple in Jerusalem, or profane, like the world outside of it. The priest further segregated the world into groups of creatures and persons who are either clean or unclean.

The heritage of the priest may be carried forward in concept and in deed. In the ancient Temple, the priest slaughtered beasts and offered them as sacrifices. In actuality, in later times, the priest may gravitate to the professions of *kashrut*—ritual slaughterer, butcher, or even assume the ritual role of circumciser, *mohel*.

In his philosophical or spiritual thought, the priest carries forward a perspective on the universe that does not set out to find a mystical precinct wherein God dwells. He already knows that God abides (or abided) in the Temple. He prefers a distant and transcendent God, rather than an imminent and mystically accessible one. He looks at the heavens to seek out the order of creation, not to find the address of the deity. Those characteristics differentiate the priest from the mystic.

As I extract what is priestly into an archetype, I add the notions that the priest naturally takes interest in other matters subsidiary to the profession of Temple functionary. He is concerned with ritual clothing and objects, calendar dates, chronologies and measurements. My constructed ideal priest-figure adheres to the value system that defined the earlier historical biblical priesthood, including those traits that I summarized.

I have formulated the definitions of the timeless priest archetype. And, now, I need to find parts of those points of view expressed in Judaic liturgy. In the corpus of classical prayers, recited for centuries by all Jews, I do find some prominent archetypal expressions of the priest's practices and beliefs.

Let's look at the theology of the priest. Our priest will not commonly seek religious meaning in terms like mercy, grace or compassion. He will recognize the reality of sin and the need for an abstract means of repentance to replace the stylized absolution of the Israelite cult.

I find this value obviously articulated in a blessing in the Amidah. I see that as the priest's main liturgy, the standing prayer, also known as the prayer of eighteen blessings:

> Forgive us, our Father, for we have sinned Pardon us, our King, for we have transgressed; for you pardon and forgive. Blessed are you, O Lord, the gracious One who repeatedly forgives. (Koren Siddur, p. 116)

Unlike the mystic, the priest takes little interest in angels or dreams. He would rather suppress these elements of spirituality that could limit his control over access to the mysteries of God. He wants to be the sole or main intermediary between the Israelite and the realm of the divine.

Our ideal priest is not partial to scribal values, such as a prayer that places its overarching value on the professional study of Torah. Likewise, he downplays the utility of *tefillin, mezuzot* or *tzitzit*—choices of emphasis and paramount value for the scribe. The Deuteronomic history takes a back seat for the priest to other expressions of Israelite virtue, especially those found in the book of Leviticus. Front and center for his worldview is the desire to know the order and meaning of the hierarchy in the Temple on Earth and in its imagined heavenly counterpart.

Several of the core blessings of the Amidah ask God to fulfill an openly priestly agenda. The fourteenth beseeches God to rebuild the city of Jerusalem and to restore the Kingdom of David:

> Return in mercy to Jerusalem your city, and dwell in it as you have promised. Rebuild it soon in our day as an eternal structure, and quickly set up in it the throne of David. Blessed are you, O Lord, who rebuilds Jerusalem.

The fifteenth blessing asks God to make flourish the descendant of King David, who will be the savior messiah:

> Speedily cause the offspring of your servant David to flourish, and let him be exalted by your saving power, for we wait all day long for your salvation. Blessed are you, O Lord, who causes salvation to flourish.

What could be more obvious? The seventeenth blessing asks God to restore the Temple and sacrificial services:

> Be pleased, O Lord our God, with your people Israel and with their prayers. Restore the service to the inner sanctuary of your Temple, and receive in love and with favor both the fire-offerings of Israel and their prayers. May the worship of your people Israel always be acceptable to you. And let our eyes behold your return in mercy to Zion. Blessed are you, O Lord, who restores his divine presence to Zion.

Finally, for the most palpable priestly indicator of all, consider that, during the public recitation of the Amidah, prior to the nineteenth blessing on holidays during the Additional Service, the descendants of the priests in the synagogue are given recognition and honor. They rise to recite the biblical priestly blessings. And on other days, when they do not physically ascend to bless the congregants in the synagogue, in the everyday recitation of the Amidah in every service, the leader inserts and recites the verses of the priestly blessing as follows:

Our God and God of our fathers, bless us with the threefold blessing in the Torah, written by the hand of Moses your servant and pronounced by Aaron and his sons the priests, your holy people, as it is said:

> May the Lord bless you and protect you.
> May the Lord make his face shine on you and be gracious to you.
> May the Lord turn his face toward you, and grant you peace. (Numbers 6)

That's another clear indication that this is the primary liturgy of the priestly archetype.

To be sure, a full parsing of the complex Amidah prayer will reveal multiple layers of expression and meaning that go beyond this core agenda of priestly values. This liturgy is not a pure expression of the values and ideas of one archetype. So I note, for instance, that a mystical angelic Kedushah found its way as an insertion into this Amidah.

[Reader] We will sanctify your name in this world just as it is sanctified in the highest heavens, as it is written by your prophet: "And they call out to one another and say:

[Cong.] 'Holy, holy, holy is the Lord of hosts; the whole earth is full of his glory.'" (Isaiah 6:3)

[Reader] Those facing them praise God saying:

[Cong.] "Blessed be the Presence of the Lord in his place." (Ezekiel 3:12)

[Reader] And in your Holy Words it is written, saying,

[Cong.] "The Lord reigns forever, your God, O Zion, throughout all generations. Hallelujah." (Psalms 146:10)

[Reader] Throughout all generations we will declare your greatness, and to all eternity we will proclaim your holiness. Your praise, O our God, shall never depart from our mouth, for you are a great and holy God and King. Blessed are you, O Lord, the holy God.

You can see that this section of the prayer is of a different character or genre than the other blessings of the Amidah. It's a responsive dramatic exchange between the reader and the congregation with citations of biblical verses that represent mystical adorations of the Lord.

Even with this mystic's prayer interlaced within it, I judge that the Amidah in essence is a priest's prayer.

It is further evident that the Amidah is not a scribe's prayer. I find it striking that the scribe's central concerns with the study of Torah and accounts of the mitzvot are not overt themes in this liturgy. As I noted in the scribe's chapter above, I was startled as well at how the Amidah's thirteenth blessing asks sardonically for compassion for "the remnant of their scribes."

> Upon the righteous, upon the pious, upon the elders of your people, the House of Israel, upon the remnant of their scribes, upon the righteous converts and upon us, may your compassion be aroused, Lord our God.

And while this may provoke some puzzlement, finally I assert that this Amidah, comprised of nineteen blessings, is not an archetypal meditator's prayer, either. But, you may legitimately inquire, did I not start this chapter with a discourse on the nature of *kavvanah*, the meditative concentration needed for the recitation of the Amidah? And you may ask further, are not blessings the basic components of the meditator's liturgical style? In my chapter on the meditator, below, I will assert that they are.

To confound matters some more, I say now that not all who meditate and recite blessings are archetypal meditators. So I need to explain here what I see as the difference between associating a style of meditating with a prayer and a full-fledged meditator's prayer. "Meditate," in the generic sense, implies a substitute, a synonym for focus, for what generically the rabbis call *kavvanah*.

All focusers or concentrators are not archetypal meditators. I'm stubbornly reserving the *meditator* label for the archetype we meet elsewhere. In my discourse on the ideal meditator-type, I will present my case that certain rabbinic blessings form a vital mode of expression for the archetypal meditator. We will see how that works soon.

I am faced with a liturgical irony. The Amidah is a prayer of nineteen blessings that does not cultivate the intrinsic meditative nature of blessings. Though blessings are the format of the liturgy, they serve as extrinsic item frames for statements of creed in the form of statements of need. They formulate a listing in request form of the doctrines of the priestly archetype. There is no way that you can convince me that these are significant components of an archetypal meditator's spiritual formations.

It will have to suffice that I say that the priestly prayer adopts the blessing as a form of expression, but not as a core of expression. The priest does not want or expect the congregation or the leader in this prayer to engage in meditation or to find instances of mindfulness or states of compassion. He expects the recitation of this prayer to bring disciplined focus onto his agenda of dogmas and to shine military-like clarity onto the articles of his faith.

Avatars of the Priest

The concept of avatar has several meanings. First, an avatar can be an embodiment or a personification of a substantial idea, for instance, "the embodiment of hope," "the incarnation of evil," "the very avatar of cunning." In some respects, what I have been describing in this book is how the prayers serve as avatars of several diverse personalities. In this sense, I can say that the Amidah is an avatar of the priest.

An avatar in the context of religions can have another meaning. In specific, it is a manifestation of a Hindu deity, particularly Vishnu, in a human, superhuman or animal form. Here is an example of how the term is used: "The Buddha is regarded as an avatar of the god Vishnu." In this sense of the term, I created my archetypal avatars, such as my "priest," as representatives of the core values that inhere in the prayers. I will expand on my variation of this sense of avatar here.

It's interesting to note in passing that the most recent technological application of the word 'avatar,' denotes a computer user's self-representation or alter ego, in the form of a three-dimensional model within a computer game, or as a two-dimensional icon picture on a screen, or as a single-dimensional username within an Internet community or in a digital game system.

To be candid, I don't have exact instances of avatars in my account of the prayers in this book or in the prayers themselves. But I do have an analogue that I want to develop with you.

On two special occasions, Hanukkah and Purim, we add paragraphs to the Amidah to describe the victories of heroic Jews of the past. I see these hero figures as avatars of the priest.

Consider this: Where are we told to insert for Hanukkah and Purim the thanksgiving prayers commemorating the heroes and miracles of those festivals? The liturgy masters could have instructed us to add the special accounts of victory anywhere in the services. But, by no coincidence, they said to add them right into the Amidah, into the blessing of Hoda'ah, thanksgiving, the eighteenth blessing.

The Hanukkah narrative glorifies an actual priest, Mattathias, and celebrates his victory of reclaiming and purifying the Temple. The prologue sentence of the prayer is used on Purim and on Israel Independence Day (for some) as well:

> And for the miracles, for the redemption, for the mighty deeds, for the saving acts, and for the wonders which you have wrought for our ancestors in those days, at this time.

For Hanukkah the prayer continues:

> In the days of Mattathias, the son of Yohanan the High Priest, the Hasmonean and his sons, when the wicked Hellenistic government rose up against your people Israel to make them forget your Torah and violate the decrees of your will. But you, in your abounding mercies, stood by them in the time of their distress. You waged their battles, defended their rights, and avenged the wrong done to them.
>
> You delivered the mighty into the hands of the weak, the many into the hands of the few, the impure into the hands of the pure, the wicked into the hands of the righteous, and the wanton sinners into the hands of those who occupy

themselves with your Torah. You made a great and holy name for yourself in your world, and brought about a great deliverance and redemption for your people Israel to this very day. Then your children entered the shrine of your house, cleansed your Temple, purified your sanctuary, kindled lights in your holy courtyards, and instituted these eight days of Hanukkah to give thanks and praise to your great name.

The inserted passage for Purim recounts and gives thanks for the deliverance at the hands of Mordecai and Esther, two leaders who also fit as historical avatars for the frequently public, and at times heroic, priest archetype.

In the days of Mordecai and Esther, in Shushan the capital, when the wicked Haman rose up against them, and sought to destroy, to slay and cause to perish all the Jews, both young and old, little children and women, on one day, on the thirteenth day of the twelfth month, which is the month Adar, and to take the spoil of them for a prey. Then you in your abundant mercy brought his counsel to nothing, frustrated his design, and returned his recompense upon his own head. And they hanged him and his sons upon the gallows.

A third proposed parallel narration (adopted by Conservative Jews but not by Orthodox) for Israel Independence Day recounts and gives thanks for the deliverance at the hands of anonymous heroes, unnamed leaders who brought forth the victories that created the State of Israel in 1948. They also fit properly among those leaders celebrated as avatars of the ideal priest.

In the days when your children were returning to their borders, at the time of a people revived in its land as in days of old, the gates to the land of our ancestors were closed before those who were fleeing the sword. When enemies from within the land together with seven neighboring nations sought to annihilate your people, you, in your great mercy, stood by them in time of trouble. You defended them and vindicated them. You gave them the courage to meet their foes, to open the gates to those seeking refuge, and to free the land of its armed invaders. You delivered the many into the hands of the few, the guilty into the hands of the

innocent. You have wrought great victories and miraculous
deliverance for your people Israel to this day, revealing your
glory and your holiness to all the world. (*Siddur Sim Shalom
for Shabbat and Festivals*, 1998, The Rabbinical Assembly,
p. 149.)

Okay, I'm bending and stretching the concept of the avatar.
Still—as I see it—the anonymous architects of the synagogue
services did a good job picking out stories of avatars of the
priestly archetype to insert into the priest's Amidah. (And to
be completely accurate, these passages are also recited outside
of the daily Amidah liturgy, when they are inserted into the
Blessings after the Meal on the respective holidays.)

I find the idea of the avatar a colorful way to visualize and
parse the sacred concepts that inhere in the liturgy. To help
you get to know more about the priest archetype, I introduce
you to two additional historical avatars. You will see how
historical images embody my virtual idea and its concepts in
these two widely disparate instances.

Eleazar and Gamaliel

Our next avatar appears as a protagonist named Eleazar
ben Azariah in an account of a dispute among ancient
rabbis.

The Talmud recounts how a priest, Rabbi Eleazar ben
Azariah, became the governing patriarch (i.e., the highest
ranking Jewish religious authority) after the rabbis deposed
the sitting patriarch, Rabban Gamaliel, on account of a
dispute about whether reciting the Amidah prayer in the
evening was compulsory or optional.

The short yet complex narrative that describes this event
intertwines politics, religion and liturgy. It illustrates how
these three dynamics interact in one brief account of a small
chapter of Jewish cultural history. The Talmudic story (Bavli
Berakhot 27b-28a) narrates how the patriarch Gamaliel was
deposed from his position.

If there is a contemporary analogue to this mini-drama,
which I will cite below, it might be a story of how a rabbi is
humiliated in his "congregation" in front of the "board of
directors" over some ostensible dispute over prayer rituals

and his "contract was not renewed." Gossip ensued, a young replacement rabbi was hustled in, but ultimately the senior rabbi regained his original position.

The Talmud narrates a dispute over whether to require Jews to recite the Amidah at night. The quarrel is between two paradigmatic public leaders. These protagonists act neither as priests of a central national Temple, nor as pretenders to a throne. They struggle over an office called Patriarch, which was held by a Jewish leader who represented the local populace in ancient Israel when the state was under Roman rule.

I have recast here the Talmud narrative as a dramatic script with a few elaborations.

> (One time a student came before R. Joshua.)
> Student: Is reciting the evening Amidah prayer optional or compulsory?
> Joshua: Optional!
> (He came before R. Gamaliel.)
> Student: Is reciting the evening Amidah prayer optional or compulsory?
> Gamaliel: Compulsory!
> Student: Did not R. Joshua say to me, 'Optional'?
> Gamaliel: I'm calling the cops. Wait until the shield bearers enter the study house.
> (When the cops entered, the inquirer stood up.)
> Student: Is reciting the evening Amidah prayer optional or compulsory?
> Gamaliel: Compulsory!
> Gamaliel (to the sages): Is there no one who disagrees in this matter?
> Joshua: No!
> Gamaliel (to Joshua): Did they not say in your name, 'Optional'?
> Gamaliel (to Joshua): Joshua, stand on your feet and they will bear witness against you.
> (Joshua stood.)
> Joshua: If I were alive and the witness dead—the living can contradict the dead. But, now that I am alive and he is alive, how can the living contradict the living?

(R. Gamaliel sat and expounded and R. Joshua stood in humiliation on his feet until the entire assembly shouted.)

Assembly (to Huspit the lecturer): Stop!

(He stopped lecturing.)

Assembly: How long will Gamaliel go on troubling him? On the last New Year he troubled him with regard to the firstling; pertaining to the incident of R. Sadoq he troubled him; here, too, he has troubled him. Let us remove him.

Whom shall we appoint in his stead? Shall we appoint R. Joshua? No, since he is party to the dispute. Shall we appoint R. Aqiva? No, he might be punished since he has no ancestral merit.

Rather we shall appoint Rabbi Eleazar ben Azariah.

For he is a sage and he is tenth in descent from Ezra. He is a sage—for if one questions him, he can answer. He is rich—if he must go pay honor to the Caesar, he too can go with authority. And he is tenth in descent from Ezra—for he has the pedigree of ancestral merit and will not be punished.

Assembly (to Eleazar): Would it please the master to head the academy?

Eleazar (to the assembly): I will go and consult the members of my household.

(He went and consulted his wife.)

Eleazar's Wife: Don't do it. They may remove you.

Eleazar: I'm going to. Let a man use a valuable cup one day and let it be broken the next.

Eleazar's Wife: You aren't an elder. You won't get respect. You have no white hair.

(On that day he was eighteen years old. A miracle befell him and eighteen rows of his hair turned white.)

This is as Rabbi Eleazar ben Azariah said, "Behold I look like I am a seventy-year-old."

This tale is a rare vignette that the Talmud preserves about the history and development of the synagogue and its prayers. I've always asked about these Talmudic records that we have, why tell us this particular story about the evening prayer? It's not a tale that teaches us how to be spiritual beings, not by any means. It's not an anecdote that illuminates the contents or meanings of the prayers. This public conflict between the priest Eleazar and the patriarch Gamaliel is about whether the community must recite the priestly Amidah at night. It tells us little or nothing about the contents or values of the liturgy.

The strange drama about a dispute over prayer unfolds in the enclosed setting of the study house, not on a national stage. It veers off to one hero's home and ends with a personal miracle.

What comes across here is a yarn about archetypal priests struggling to assert their roles of leadership to govern. The realm over which these leaders rule is the domain of the synagogue and the extrinsic details of how people ought to pray. And consider that this is an episode of internecine bickering. It is not a particularly flattering story. Yet, the inheritors of the tradition saw fit to canonize it and make it part of the Talmudic record. It illuminates one imagined setting in which you learn about the struggles of the priestly archetypes that you meet in the synagogue.

Finally, note that both Eleazar and Gamaliel agreed that it is compulsory to recite the evening prayer. I do not know the actual reasons for the removal of Gamaliel from his position. The ostensible explanation and the upshot of the story is that he was deposed because the congregation disliked him. He humiliated his peers. Arguing in the synagogue is tolerated. But, in such an enclosed and intimate social setting, overbearing acts of humiliation are not permitted.

The story tells us that there once was a serious breach of the priest's discipline in the synagogue but it was resolved and order and authority were restored.

Amidah Phenomena

The final avatar of the priest that I discuss actually is an original category in a modern historian's observations about Jews who acted heroically in the Holocaust.

This inspiring articulation of the priest archetype emerges from a remarkable insight by historian Yehuda Bauer. He borrowed a liturgical term to describe certain types of valiant community leadership and behavior during the awful events of the Holocaust during the Second World War.

In his perceptive works of history, first in his book *Rethinking the Holocaust* and then continued in *The Death of the Shtetl,* Bauer tells the tragic story of the eradication—off the face of the earth—of the small Jewish towns in Europe, known as *shtetls.* Bauer's work provides a definitive and focused closure for us on this topic.

I had read previously different and somewhat romanticized portrayals of the European *shtetl.* The historians Mark Zbrowski and Elizabeth Herzog, in their well-known book, *Life is with People,* constructed a picture of an ideal world of collective camaraderie in the small Jewish towns of Europe. And, of course, a thoroughly romantic version of *shtetl* life comes across in the Broadway version of that culture in the popular play *Fiddler on the Roof,* based on the work of the European writer Sholem Aleichem.

In his contrasting, meticulously documented, vivid and argumentative manner, Yehuda Bauer gives us his historian's angle on the story. He explains how the *shtetls* of the *kresy* region in Eastern Poland were weakened by the Russians and then eliminated by the Germans. "By the end of 1942, most of the shtetlach in the kresy had been decimated... By early 1943 the shtetlach had been annihilated..." (Bauer, *The Death of the Shtetl,* p. 67).

Bauer inquires and probes into how history unfolded for the *shtetls.* He reconstructs the tense and dramatic events of the past.

When you get to his discussion about Jewish resistance, you realize that Bauer invented his own term for describing the resistance of some of the Jews against the onslaught of the Nazis. Bauer could have labeled it resistance, battle, defiance, struggle, challenge or by any number of other terms. He chose instead to call the phenomenon, "Amidah."

Here is how Bauer describes the phenomenon he calls Amidah in his book, *Rethinking the Holocaust*:

> The Hebrew term amidah...means literally "standing up against," but that does not capture the deeper sense of the word. When I speak of resistance, I mean amidah, and that includes both armed and unarmed actions and excludes passive resistance, although that term is almost a non sequitur, because one cannot really resist passively. When one refuses to budge in the face of brutal force, one does not

resist passively; one resists without using force, and that is not the same thing.

What does amidah include? It includes smuggling food into ghettos; mutual self-sacrifice within the family to avoid starvation or worse; cultural, educational, religious and political activities taken to strengthen morale; the work of doctors, nurses and educators to consciously maintain health and moral fiber to enable individual and group survival; and, of course, armed rebellion or the use of force (with bare hands or with 'cold' weapons) against the Germans and their collaborators. (*Rethinking the Holocaust*, p. 120.)

In the discussion in his later book, *The Death of the Shtetl,* he notes that, "Unarmed Amidah in the kresy was limited by the impossible external circumstances, although it did exist in some places and was expressed in ways that were specific to the areas discussed here." In his earlier volume, the word "Amidah" is in lowercase, but in this subsequent work he capitalizes *Amidah*, imputing to it some additional symbolic significance.

I find Bauer's adoption of the term Amidah meaningful because I, above, identified the priest archetype of the synagogue with the rabbinic Amidah prayer. The identifiable behavior during the epoch of the Holocaust, which Bauer labels Amidah, fits well with the public leadership personality pattern of our present archetype.

I relate this to my archetypal analysis in two ways. First, it makes me associate the standing prayer called the Amidah with the resistance to tyranny, also called the Amidah. Second, it makes me observe that the priest archetype, which you met in this chapter, may also represent a community's staunch leader, a person of discipline whose main goal is to uphold and defend the community institutions and their public structures.

Strikingly then, through his intuitive grasp of the reality of Jewish experience, the great historian Yehuda Bauer called communal resistance during the trying era of the Holocaust, the Amidah. And those heroes of the Amidah, whom he chronicled, represent the best of the essence of our priest archetype in the experience of Jewish cultural destiny.

My Father's Formal Synagogue

Praying and the synagogue were central to my life from my early childhood. My father, Zev Zahavy, was the rabbi of several distinguished New York City synagogues on the West Side and then the East Side of Manhattan.

When he was at Congregation Zichron Ephraim, I recall many times accompanying him to his work on 67th Street, off Third Avenue. His rabbi's study in the synagogue was a quiet, private room off to the side of the main sanctuary. My dad kept it lined with books and it was filled with a musty smell. The building dated back to the 1800's and the hallway to the study had the creakiest wood floor I ever walked on.

Although our family was not descended from the priests, my father, better than anyone else I know, appreciated the formality of ritual and the probity of the agenda of the priestly archetype of prayer. At that time, his synagogue in Manhattan was a stately place with formal services, led by a professional *hazzan*. At Sabbath and holiday services, my dad wore a robe and high hat—a black one during the year and a white one on the High Holy Days. As he sat in his high-backed chair up on the elevated seat at the front of the sanctuary beside the ark of the Torahs, he looked like a priest officiating in the Temple in Jerusalem.

My dad also was famous in the city for his sermons. He labored over them for hours. To let them know about what he planned to be preaching on Saturday, every Wednesday he sent "releases" of his coming sermons to the local papers, such as the *NY Times, Herald Tribune, Journal American* and others. Those were the 1950s and the *Times* and other papers covered as news the important Saturday and Sunday sermons that were delivered in the city. Frequently, we'd look around the sanctuary to see if the reporter from the *Times* or another paper was present. We'd know because he'd be the person sitting in the back of the *shul* and writing feverishly on his reporter's pad—something that the congregants don't do in the synagogue on the Sabbath.

For my dad, in honor of his ninetieth birthday, I collected and made a book out of the 230 summaries, reports and citations of his rabbinic speeches that were published in the *Times*. If you page through the topics of those sermons, you'll see a reflection of the priestly agenda of the Amidah, ranging from the topics of the return to Israel and Jerusalem, to ethics and morality, to health and welfare and to world peace. His sermon topics were never distractions from the synagogue prayers. While they always related to contemporary affairs, they consistently drew from and embodied the main Jewish values at the core of the prayers. They extended and validated the themes of the liturgy.

My father was especially ambitious about increasing the attendance at the services. We his children had to count the number of people in *shul* and discuss that at the Shabbat lunch table. Then he'd ask us how the sermon was and we all answered enthusiastically every week, "It was terrrrrrific!"

High points of my childhood were oft times linked to Jewish holidays and to the *shul*. The Simchat Torah holiday was especially great. On that one day, I was permitted to ascend to the *bimah* and sit in my father's velvet-covered chair. In those days, that was considered a wild thing to allow a child to do, especially in such a formal sanctuary.

On Pesach night, hundreds of congregants attended the big collective public Seder in the social hall at our *shul*. Our family flanked my father in seats on the elevated dais as he conducted the Seder. As a kid, I loved this Seder, mainly because of the real seltzer bottles that we had at the meal. There was nothing in the world that tasted better than a good little serving of Concord grape juice or wine with a solid shpritz of seltzer. And by the end of the night we were shpritzing each other with seltzer! When the time came to return the *afikomen*, the hidden matza that I had found, I always had a demand for a rather large and expensive toy, which my father naturally publicly promised to get me. I always did get an official *afikomen* present later—but rarely the one I asked for.

My dad managed in this setting to make parts of the scribal family Seder into a more formal priestly ritual. His intuitive mastery of the synagogue service allowed him to mediate among the archetypal styles and to create services that amalgamated the elements into smooth, balanced and meaningful ritual and worship.

He was a great performer as a rabbi in his synagogue. He embodied the priestly ideal archetype in his leadership of rituals and in his writings and orations in sermons. He went beyond that to explore the issues of the mystic archetype in books he wrote about the Kabbalah. He also pondered philosophical issues of human destiny in the universe and wrote about cosmology in a scribal mode of discourse in his other books and essays.

It was naturally expected, but never articulated, that when I grew up I'd become a *shul* rabbi. I prepared for that career all the way through ordination at Yeshiva University. But, then, I found another closely related calling. I became a professor of Judaism, rather than a synagogue rabbi. That way, I emulated somewhat my dad's calling and continued my family's involvement in Jewish learning.

I've cared about Jewish prayer all of my life. I've written ten books about Jewish texts and rituals, mostly about prayer and praying. The motivations behind my choice of topics of my academic scholarly research and for writing this more popular book were inspired by all the experiences of my childhood and especially influenced by my veneration of my father, Rabbi Zev Zahavy—a man of proper priestly demeanor, mystical imagination, scribal interests, an actor's talents, a celebrity's prominence and meditative graces.

The Meditator's Prayers

BE·RA·KHAH
[*Seph.* bRah-**KHah**; *Ashk.* **bRaw**-KH*uh*]
—*noun, plural* [*Seph.* -**KHawt**], -khos *Ashk.* -xəz [*Ashk.* -KH*uh*z]. *Hebrew.*
a blessing or benediction, usually recited according to a traditional formula.
Also, berakah, berachah.
Origin: Heb bərākhāh

—Random House Dictionary, 2010

*D*eborah sits in the synagogue visibly engaged in her prayers. She closes her eyes at times. She sways as she prays, rhythmically and persistently, but slowly, gently and with deliberation.

You cannot tell just from these external cues that Deborah is a meditator. To know that, I need to probe and ask her about her innermost thoughts during her time in the synagogue and at many other times when she is out and about throughout the day. During her prayers, you need to know, is Deborah attentively introspective of her own needs and desires and those of her friends and loved ones? Does she see her dreams fulfilled? Is she accepting of her personal and spiritual shortcomings and failures? Is she aware of her own breathing and heartbeat and the air that swirls around her, the heft of her Siddur and the humming of her fellow daveners?

Does Deborah recite one-hundred daily blessings with mindful recognition? Does she reach a state of compassion as she says the grace over her meals?

I might describe the activity of meditation as "study or thinking intently and at length, as for spiritual purposes," or as "contemplation of spiritual matters."

But the ancient rabbis did not have a term to describe meditation, so they called the meditative dimension of prayer, "the service of the heart." To them, that indicated an inner intellectual and emotional activity, which they located in the heart, since they could detect that as the organ which beats slower or faster depending on one's state of mind. Ancient rabbis had no ideas of brain activity and surely had no devices to monitor it or methods to speak about it.

Today, there are indeed multiple ways that we use the term *meditate* to describe a person who practices *meditation* through a variety of activities that we may call *meditative.* It's enough to make your head spin. Before I get to what goes on in and around the synagogue, consider for instance those meditators from the 1960s or 70s, who practiced a popular form of Transcendental Meditation (TM), Zen or other related types of meditation. Far outside of establishment places of worship—separate from synagogues and churches—they sought a regimen that would help them achieve a sensation that they could transcend or go beyond themselves. They sought to bend their consciousness by a variety of methods, such as by finding their mantra or via deliberation on gnomic Zen sayings, called *koans.*

The rapid spread in popularity of TM back then frightened organized religion. Some rabbis specifically declared it to be a forbidden form of idolatry. In 1978, the Lubavitcher Rebbe railed against the threats of meditative cults on the one hand, while on the other hand he called for Jewish doctors to develop a kosher form of therapeutic meditation. By that, he meant they should come up with an independent new course of meditative exercises within Jewish practice and based on Jewish principles or contents.

The rebbe's suggestion about meditation has not much to do with what we are talking about. I have come here with you now—to the synagogue service—to present to you Deborah the meditator so you can get to know her. As I have learned in my own travels and quests, for Deborah, there is no reason to exit the synagogue or to abandon standard Jewish practices in order to discover ways to meditate. Deborah practices meaningful meditation at the core of her regular standard Jewish prayer and in her daily life through the ordinary texts and actions of her Jewish living.

Now, it is true that the rich meditative qualities of regular Jewish practice were not at all self-evident to me or to Deborah, at first. No Jewish teacher instructed her about them. She reached her understanding and practices through a journey of discovery, all her own and in several stages.

Deborah, at one time, went through a stressful period in her life. She sought ways and means to deal with her overwhelming, swirling anxieties that carried her through flights of manic euphoria to bouts of dark depression. She tried many techniques to take back control of her runaway consciousness. Fortunately, among them, Deborah trained in a course of mindfulness meditation, a derivative of Buddhist practices that seeks to foster clear awareness for an individual of the sensations of their present physical and mental state as it unfolds in the present moment.

As a mindful meditator, Deborah learned to observe more vividly the place she was in—the tones, shades, gradations and nuances of her present, her immediate exterior reality and the flowing progression of her inner thoughts and emotions.

She discovered, in the course of her training, one of the best-selling and most perceptive books on mindful meditation, a volume by Jon Kabat-Zinn, one of its leading proponents in the U.S. That book was *Wherever You Go, There You Are*. Now, although Kabat-Zinn is a Jew, he has no identifiable connections to Judaism. His insights are derived in the main from Eastern religions and practices. Deborah had to make all the connections back to her practices of Judaism on her own.

Over time, wherever Deborah went, including the synagogue, she became an accomplished mindful meditator. Deborah was able to moderate her own thoughts; to stand outside of them and observe the flow of her consciousness going by, much like a naturalist might observe the currents of a river.

When she came into the synagogue after training as a mindful meditator, Deborah started to find analogues to that style of meditation in the existing practices of her established Jewish rituals.

Accordingly, let's see how Deborah embodies them as our synagogue archetype—the meditator—the practitioner of mindful blessings and intercessions of compassion.

On entering the synagogue as a meditator, Deborah realized that she was a practitioner of the meditations that we call blessings or, in Hebrew, *berakhot*. Deborah breathtakingly discovered new dimensions of her old prayers.

She found that a blessing is more than a formula of Hebrew words that have simple knowable meanings. In the past, she had thought that the fixed opening phrase of a *berakhah*, "Blessed art thou O Lord, our God, King of the Universe," semantically expressed the speaker's intention to bestow good wishes upon God or to exalt God, who is referred to in the formula by three names. Deborah learned this formula when she was two or three years old and hardly pondered the theological meaning or even the simple semantics of this phrase each time she recited it as an older child or as an adult.

So what new purpose or function of the *berakhah* formula did Deborah discover when she came back to reexamine it as a mature meditator? She saw that these recitations served for her as the known cues for many instances of her daily, periodic, repetitive or occasional mini-mindful meditations. These provided for Deborah meaningful guidance to the rush of her thoughts and to the meanderings of the awareness of her waking life.

Deborah the meditator recited her individual blessings when she ate her foods, performed her bodily functions, witnessed meteorological events, saw flowers, or heard good and bad news. She also recited blessings when she suspended the routines that maintained her daily subsistence and when she broke off from the flow of her living in the external world, that is, when she went off into the synagogue to engage in her hours of prayer.

Here is a tabular summary of a small sample of many of the actions and occasions for which Deborah recited her mini-meditations, the blessings in her daily activities:

Blessed are You...	Purpose	Meditation
Who creates the fruit of the tree	Before eating a fruit	Mindful eating
Who creates the produce of the ground	Before eating a vegetable	Mindful eating
Who gives pleasant fragrance to fruits	Upon smelling fruits	Mindful sensing of nature
Who has withheld nothing from nature and has created in it beautiful creatures and trees for the enjoyment of human beings	Upon seeing flowering trees in their first seasonal bloom	Mindful sensing of the special beauty of nature
Who creates the fruit of the vine	Before drinking wine	Mindful drinking
Who brings forth bread from the earth	Before eating bread— a full meal	Mindful dining, for a full meal
Who commanded us to light the Sabbath/ holiday candles	After lighting the candles	Purposeful ritual, mindful of the passage of time
Who heals all flesh and performs wonders	After bathroom visits	Mindful of one's body and health
Whose power and might fill the world	Upon witnessing thunder or a hurricane	Mindful of disruptive events of nature
Who is good and does good	For good news	Mindful of elevating emotions
Who is the true judge	For bad news	Mindful of emotional trauma
Blessings in the synagogue	Opening or concluding paragraphs of liturgy	Mindful of the markers of the elements of prayer

There are three generally mentioned classical categories for sorting out all the blessings: (1) blessings of performance of a mitzvah (ritual acts), (2) blessings of bodily satisfaction (intake of foods, drinks, etc.) and (3) blessings of praise (liturgy).

As part of her mindful practice, these blessings functioned to demand of Deborah a meditative awareness of her person, her body and her immediate external world. For a simple example, she took the blessing she recites upon smelling fragrant fruit, "Blessed are You, Lord our God, King of the Universe who gives pleasant fragrance to fruits" (Koren Siddur, p. 1000) as a cue to be highly aware of her surroundings. She took another case, the formula she spoke before eating an apple, "Blessed are You, Lord our God, King of the Universe who creates the fruit of the tree," as a cue to mindfully savor the taste and texture of her foods. In both cases, aspects of loving-kindness and compassion accompanied the awareness of the physical food.

These blessings served as triggers for Deborah. They told her to stop, to be mindful of her actions, to be thoughtful of what type of food she held in her hand, how that food was to be regarded and classified, whether she was smelling it or eating it, and to recall what is "its correct *berakhah*."

All forms of mindfulness heighten the practitioner's moments of experience and elevate ordinary events from a background of awareness to a foreground of thinking. For Deborah, mindful occasions of blessings helped her savor her conscious awareness—the consistency and flavor, the origins and essences of her living.

Meir, a rabbi in the Talmud in the second century, spoke of his expectation for every Jew to experience each day one-hundred triggers of mindful meditation—a life punctuated daily by one-hundred blessings.

To be clear, this mindful meditation through *berakhot* that we have described is not identical to that which Kabat-Zinn and others taught Deborah. She had to adapt her mindfulness to apply it to her Jewish context. In fact, Deborah realized that, through her blessings, she engaged in mindfulness to the second power, to mindfulness squared, that is to a heightened relationship to her multiple worlds, both personal and cultural. Let me explain.

Deborah understood that, when she held an apple in her hand and recited the blessing for it, she had to know which proper *berakhah* to make. That meant she had to relate first to that content from her cultural world, Jewish tradition, law or *halakhah*. Still holding that apple in her hand, she moved through that relationship to look then at the fruit, to feel its heft and taste its tartness as she bit into it.

Because she was mindful, Deborah's interaction with daily life was not defined just by the torrents of her rushing thoughts. Her thinking was formed in a duplex relationship to that combination of both the cultural and personal contents that she mindfully activated in her conscious mind, under her watchful control. She steered her relationship to her own thoughts and actions by meeting up with them, by making note of them, and then by becoming disentangled from those twisting currents of distractions gushing around her life.

Deborah's blessing-meditations turned the rush of her daily living into a series of discrete moments of experience, each savored fully with thanksgiving, gratitude and, perhaps, with compassion.

I hedge regarding compassion because it's likely that Deborah learned more, at first, about the practice of compassion outside of the Judaic framework. True, the cultivation of loving-kindness and compassion is a part of Judaism. However, embracing those who are distressed and feeling the pain of others is more of a core doctrine of Buddhism and, along with it, a prominent part of its meditative practices.

That said, as we discuss below, the grace after meals stands out as a prominent example of a prayer and meditation of compassion, and it is squarely within the practice of Judaism.

What more do we understand about the meditation of the recitation of a blessing? By convention, because a blessing invokes three names of a divine entity ("Blessed are You, Lord our God, King of the Universe..."), classical Judaism says that it accomplishes something we conventionally describe as the *sanctification* of the acts that the meditator performs after each blessing. By her actions of reciting a blessing and then eating, for instance, Deborah fulfilled a commandment. Deborah knows and observes this added explanation of her practice. This is part of the external cultural baggage that she brings to bear on the other essential elements of her mindful actions.

Deborah's Jewish application of mindful meditation stands somewhat apart from the mindfulness that derives from Buddhist sources and has wended its way into our American cultural setting. Let's look at an illustration to clarify better how it differs.

Deborah has a friend Tara who practices mindful meditation anchored in a Buddhist tradition. For this demonstration, let's imagine that both meditators pick up a raisin to eat, to demonstrate their ways of meditation.

This mindful raisin-eating exercise is actually practiced to instruct beginners in the goals and modes of Kabat-Zinn's style of mindfulness. In the Kabat-Zinn mindful exercise, the leader hands each beginner a single raisin and asks the person to eat it. Most ordinary people will pop the raisin in their mouths, chew a few times and swallow it, largely unconsciously.

But Tara, the meditative eater, wants to perform a mindful raisin-eating. She begins by looking closely at the raisin, considering its shape, weight, color and texture. Next, she places the raisin in her mouth and focuses on how it feels on her tongue and how her mouth responds with salivation.

Then our mindful raisin-eater chews the raisin slowly and thoroughly, focusing on its taste and disintegration. Finally, she swallows the raisin and feels it (or imagines it) as it goes down her alimentary canal and into her stomach.

While eating, Tara may find her thoughts wander to picture the red Sun-Maid raisin box that she knows held the food, or to the supermarket where she last bought a box of raisins, or perhaps to the time she found an old box of dried raisins in the bottom of her purse. But, in each case, she let her thoughts come into her mind and allowed herself to make note of them and let them go, returning her focus to eating that single, present piece of food.

Now, let's turn by comparison to consider our meditator Deborah, acting as our mindful *berakhah* raisin-eater. There's no actual single meditative exercise that Deborah knows of in Judaism comparable to what we described for the mindful raisin-eater. When children learn about reciting blessings for foods, they learn to associate the blessing that applies to each food category and to each specific food.

Let us imagine, then, this example of the way that Deborah, the meditator, would practice a *berakhah* raisin-eating mindful exercise.

Deborah first takes the raisin and looks at its size. She wants to make sure that it big enough—more than the minimum quantity—to merit that she, the eater, recites a blessing. But she knows that she must recite a blessing before eating any quantity, according to most accepted practices. Still, she needs to think ahead about how much she must eat before she is obliged to recite a blessing after eating, the blessings of the grace after a meal.

Deborah the meditator also has to decide what species of food this is—where it came from, what category it falls into—and thereby to determine the proper *berakhah* to recite before putting it into her mouth and eating it. A raisin comes from a grape and a grape grows on a vine. She may think then that the blessing should be, "who creates the fruit of the vine," but that blessing is reserved for wine, the ultimate and finest product of the grapevine.

A grape itself is the fruit of a tree—by its conventional classification. So, she concludes that its blessing is, "who creates the fruit of the tree." Deborah reflects that this food is processed from grapes. It is dried, not fresh; does that affect its blessing? She ponders, does that change it and downgrade the blessing to the most generic formula, "for all was created at his word?"

You can see that Deborah, in the Jewish context, must supply more than Tara's simple and present consideration of the physical nature of the food to her mindful-*berakhah*-raisin-eating simulation. It's not just that she must be mindful, but it becomes clear that she needs to become mindful *to a greater degree*, to a mathematically higher power, to be culturally analytical, almost botanical or culinary or scientific, religiously cognizant—all before she recites the blessing and puts the raisin in her mouth.

During this exercise, Deborah may also consider the times she forgot to recite the blessing, the confusion she felt when she did not know a blessing for a food. She may think about whether the red Sun-Maid box has a kosher certification on it, whether foods of this sort need to be certified. But, as a *mindful-berakhah* meditator, she has to bring her consciousness back to the act of eating and the heightened mode of awareness that she brings to add to that biological ingestion.

For Deborah the meditator, this deep interaction between cultural mindfulness and personal physical mindfulness defines the dynamics of her *berakhah* meditations.

Meditative Compassion

But, wait. That is not the end of our introduction of Deborah as our meditator. There is another level of meditation in her spiritual arsenal that she wants you to know about. The mindful meditation spoken of above has within it an element of meditators seeking personal compassion for themselves. In the course of her spiritual and meditative journey, Deborah learned about a more extensive type of mindful meditation.

She learned of the ethical and moral principles of non-harming, of compassion and of wisdom—consciousness that she could stimulate and recall through her mindfulness meditation practice.

Deborah learned to sit and engage in meditations of loving-kindness and compassion for the suffering of others, of sympathetic joy and equanimity. She worked hard to develop her skillful mental states and to discharge her unskillful conditions of mind.

Through meditative practices, she mastered more advanced aspects of a mindfulness-based stress-reduction for her personal well-being. And, when she applied this to her Jewish practices, she gradually saw how this training gave her new insight into her familiar religious machinery.

In her exercises of mindful loving-kindness, she would repeat the generic goals from that context that she wished for herself and for others, and then elaborate on each one:

> May I be free from danger.

May I have mental happiness.
May I have physical happiness.
May I have ease of well-being.

When she turned her attention again to the Judaic prayer of the Birkat Hamazon, the grace after meals, Deborah understood for the first time that she already practiced on a regular basis, not only so many standard mini-meditations through her blessings but also some full expressions of meditations of loving-kindness, compassion, joy and equanimity for all living beings.

When she said the words of this grace and felt their meanings, she created for herself a full exercise of compassionate meditation that brought with it the expected peace and equanimity that she sought for herself and for others.

Deborah saw that, when she recited the Birkat Hamazon, she spoke a composite prayer whose main purpose was to enunciate the grace and compassion that God bestows in stages upon those who have eaten a meal, upon the household in which they ate, upon all Israelites, and upon the entire world. Seeing clearly the meaning of the repeated invocation of God as "The merciful one," it was immediately clear to Deborah that this was a full Jewish meditation of compassion.

Here is the text of the Birkat Hamazon, the Grace after Meals:

> We praise you, God, Ruler of the universe, Who sustains the entire world with goodness, kindness and mercy. God gives food to all creatures, for God's love is everlasting. Through God's abundant goodness we have never been in want; may we never be in want of sustenance for the sake of God's great Name. God sustains all, does good to all, and provides food for all of the creatures whom God has created. We praise you, God, Who provides food for all.
>
> We thank you for having given a lovely, good and spacious land to our fathers; for having liberated us from the land of Egypt and freed us from the house of bondage; for your covenant which you have sealed in our flesh, for the Torah which you have taught us; for the laws which you have made known to us; for the life, grace and loving kindness which you have bestowed upon us, and for the

sustenance with which you nourish and maintain us continually, in every day, every season, and every hour.

For all of this, God, we thank you and praise you. May your name be praised by every living being forever, as it is written in the Torah: "When you have eaten and are satisfied, praise God for the good land which God has given you." We praise you, God, for the land and its nourishment.

… May you continue to provide us with grace, kindness, and compassion, providing us with deliverance, prosperity and ease, life and peace, and all goodness. May we never go in want of goodness.

May the Merciful One reign over us forever and ever.
May the Merciful One be extolled in heaven and on earth.
May the Merciful One be praised in every generation and be glorified through us to all eternity, and be honored among us forever.
May the Merciful One give us an honorable livelihood.
May the Merciful One break the yoke of our exile off of our necks and lead us in dignity to our land.

May the Merciful One send abundant blessing to this house and to the table at which we have eaten. May the Merciful One send us Eliyahu the prophet, of blessed memory, who will bring us good tidings of deliverance and comfort…

May our merit and the merit of our ancestors secure lasting peace for all of us. May we receive a blessing from God, and justice from the God of our salvation. May we find grace and favor in the sight of God and humans…

Revere God, you who are God's holy ones. For those who revere God suffer no want. Those who seek God will not lack anything that is good. Give thanks to God, for God is good; God's loving-kindness endures forever. Open your hand and satisfy every living thing with favor.

Blessed are those who trust in God, and God will become their security. I was young, I have grown older and I have not seen the righteous forsaken, nor their children begging for bread. May God grant strength to God's people and bless God's people with peace…

Indeed, Deborah recalls how she rejoiced when first she recognized that her own Birkat Hamazon was indeed an ideal instance of truly compassionate meditation.

Meditative Triggers

Deborah learned in her meditative training that the practitioners of Kabat-Zinn mindfulness speak of how a person ought to develop a dozen mindful triggers to reign in and direct the undisciplined flow of her consciousness throughout the day. The meditative guides propose, for example, that a person might commit to using as mindfulness triggers such everyday actions as finishing a phone call, sipping a cup of a beverage or eating snacks, starting and stopping their car, or petting their pet. These help a practitioner integrate mindfulness into his or her way of life.

For Deborah, these triggers are already prevalent and predetermined in her Jewish lifestyle. All she had to do was to recognize them for what they are. The Talmud speaks of a person reciting a panoply of one-hundred blessings each day. Deborah could choose to think of these as triggers of mindful meditations, much as the ancient Talmudic passage below suggests:

> R. Meir used to say, "There is no person is Israel who does not perform one-hundred commandments each day [and recite blessings for them].
>
> "One recites the Shema and recites blessings before and after it.
>
> "And one eats his bread and recites blessings before and after.
>
> "And one recites the Prayer of Eighteen Blessings three times.
>
> "And one performs all the other commandments and recites blessings for them." (Tosefta Berakhot 6:24)

For Deborah, the meditator's *berakhah* formulary thus has an impressive life of its own in the complex world inside the synagogue. The *berakhah* formulary serves as a conventional template for all kinds of prayers and many instances of blessings. The blessings of her daily life surrounding the synagogue also serve as the triggers and direct meditations of her mindfulness and compassion.

She contemplated though, as she looked more closely at them, that all synagogue blessings may not serve so flawlessly and identically in that capacity as meditations. In particular, she recalled the Amidah, the main prayer of the priest archetype. She asked whether the use of nineteen stylized blessing paragraphs in this composition also help to constitute a serious meditation of mindfulness. She came up with unclear and contradictory answers to that question. On the one hand, she knew that the priestly Amidah prayer demands of the participant a special *kavvanah* of discipline, from the first word of its recitation to the last.

The person reciting the Amidah already has committed to a meditative state, from the moment she starts to recite the liturgy, to ignore even a snake coiled to strike at her heel. Those nineteen *berakhot,* then, do not serve to create mindful triggers to an agenda within a vortex of daily distractions.

Deborah mulled that, perforce it is just accidental, not essential, that the blessing formulary was used as an extrinsic framework in the Amidah. It served in the prayer as a familiar means of assembling that sacred wish-list of the societal values and needs that accord with a priest's archetypal worldviews.

Or, Deborah thought, perhaps—alternatively—the blessing formulary served to break each item in the prayer into its own heightened mindful expression, to help create a focus on the main point of each element. By that claim, she concluded that there are more complex and varied ways that *kavvanah* and mindful meditation may be formed and practiced by the people we meet in our synagogue.

She knew about the prayerful focus of Rav Aharon, the scribe, and of Mr. Cohen, the priest, and she now wondered about the varieties of Jewish meditation.

She concluded that, in those two instances, people practice what we might call a kind of traffic-cop meditation. That guides a person's focus for their prayers, steers the rush of their thoughts and gives them direction—in Hebrew, *kivun.*

For Rav Aharon, the scribe's *kavvanah* is the focus of the writer at his desk. The Shema prayer is recited while seated, the normal posture of the scribe. The Mishnah makes clear that *kavvanah* for the Shema expects you to simulate a focus on textual work.

Deborah reminded us that the Mishnah text conveyed this by asking and answering its own queries about whether one may interrupt his recitation of the Shema between the paragraphs or within the paragraphs, to return a greeting or to extend a greeting. These matters were the same as those faced, as a rule, by a scribe or scholar sitting engaged in writing.

> "At the breaks between the paragraphs of the Shema one may extend a greeting to his associate out of respect, and respond to a greeting which was extended to him."
>
> "And in the middle of reciting a paragraph one may extend a greeting out of fear and respond," the words of R. Meir.
>
> R. Judah says, "In the middle of a paragraph one may extend a greeting out of fear and respond out of respect.
>
> "At the breaks between the paragraphs one may greet out of respect and respond to the greetings of any man." (Mishnah Berakhot 2:1)

Deborah observed as well that, for Mr. Cohen, the priest's *kavvanah* is the discipline of the priest at his station. She saw that the priest archetype's *kavvanah* takes cognizance of consciousness—but not as a fulfillment of serenity in this world, of the peace of God, or of a compassion for sentient beings. True to the archetype, the priest requires a meditation of discipline and obedience for the recitation of the Amidah— a martial kind of self-possession.

She reminded us that the Mishnah prescribes that, during her recitation of the Amidah prayer, even if a serpent is coiled around her heel, a person shall not pause her recitation. That means that the priestly-meditator must be in authority, in control of her emotions and consciousness. To some of us, this obligatory ritual action may sound like a form of arrogant discipline. It may seem like the polar opposite of the type of consciousness that one needs to become a mindful or compassionate meditator.

Deborah reminded us that we also know of Hannah, the mystic archetype, and we've encountered the mystic's mode of *kavvanah*. That was yet another kind of redirection of focus, different from that of the meditator, scribe or priest. The mystic pulls her focus away from this moment, from her physical synagogue on this Earth, and turns her consciousness to a distant realm in heaven.

Deborah emphasized the distinction between her practice as a meditator and that of Hannah the mystic. The mystic assembles knowledge of other times and places so she can visualize that she is somewhere else. She mostly seeks to know the mysterious, that which has meaning, which is not utterly plain to her senses or instantly perceptible to her intelligence and which is outside of her day-to-day understanding.

Acting as an archetype of the mindful meditator, Deborah reminded us that, along the way, in her spiritual journey, she had learned through her meditation and prayer, how to more vividly observe the reality of the place she was in, which she put into practice. Deborah learned how better to find both compassion and peace in the here and now of her Judaism, in her daily routine in general, and within the diverse prayers of the synagogue, surely in some of God's favorite prayers.

The Celebrity's Prayers

ALEINU

(Hebrew: עָלֵינוּ, "upon us") or Aleinu leshabei'ach ("[it is] upon us to praise [God]"), meaning "it is upon us or it is our obligation or duty to praise God." A Jewish prayer recited at the end of each of the three daily services. It is also recited following the New Moon blessing and after a circumcision is performed.

—Wikipedia, Aleinu

My quest for perfect prayer and for spiritual insights evolved, not just at synagogues on the ground but also one time during my *davening* on a jumbo jet flight at an altitude of 39,000 feet and a speed of 565 miles per hour. That is where, by happenstance on an airplane in 1982, I met Rabbi Meir Kahane, an American-Israeli Orthodox rabbi, an ultra-nationalist writer and political figure and, later, a member of the Israeli Knesset.

I recognized Kahane right away when I saw him on the flight. He was a famous New York Jew. In the 1960s and 70s, Kahane had organized the Jewish Defense League (JDL). Its goal was to protect Jews in New York City's high-crime neighborhoods and to instill Jewish pride. Kahane also was active in the struggle for the rights of Soviet Jews to emigrate from Russia and to immigrate to Israel. By 1969, he was proposing emergency Jewish mass-immigration to Israel because of the imminent threat he saw of a second Holocaust in an anti-Semitic United States. He argued that Israel be made into a state modeled on Jewish religious law, that it annex the West Bank and Gaza Strip and that it urge all Arabs to voluntarily leave Israel or to be ejected by force.

It was then, by coincidence, that I traveled with Kahane on a long Tower Air flight to Israel. As was common on flights to Israel, a few hours after takeoff, Jewish men gathered at the back of the plane. As the sun became visible in the Eastern sky, they formed a minyan, kind of an ad hoc synagogue. In this unusual and somewhat mystical setting, I prayed the morning services with the rabbi and others at the back of the jumbo jet.

After that service, I introduced myself and, during the continuation of the flight, engaged him in conversation, politely challenging Kahane at length about his radical political views. After meeting him on the plane, I followed his political career with some interest.

Kahane was a hardened nationalist. In 1984, he became a member of the Knesset representing his Kach party. In 1988, the Israeli government banned Kach as racist. On November 5, 1990, at age 58, after delivering a speech that warned American Jews to emigrate to Israel before it was too late, Kahane was assassinated in Manhattan by an Arab gunman. In 1994, Kach was outlawed in Israel and listed by the U.S. State Department as a terrorist organization.

Bearing all of this in mind, in my discussion of the celebrity-monotheist archetype of the synagogue, I call my illustrative character Rabbi Meir.

Let me introduce you to Rabbi Meir, the celebrity-monotheist. First, let me tell you how he differs from my five other synagogue friends.

Rabbi Meir is not much of a scribe. He is not happy just to sit at his desk with his books, to keep track of his texts and accounts. He is a man in motion, expecting change in the world at large, provoking it where he can and watching for it all the time.

Rabbi Meir is not much of priest, either. He cares, but not a lot, for the priestly content, the values we associate with the Temple, the precincts of the sacred or the profane, the lineages and classifications of the kosher and *treif*. But he does cast himself very much like the priest in one respect: He visualizes his role as a designated high profile leader of his people with a clearly specified public mission.

Rabbi Meir is not a meditative type of person anchored in the immediate textures of this world of ours, here in the synagogue building. He is not much of a mystic either, seeking flights of ascent to know the intimacies of heaven.

Rabbi Meir is not a well-rounded mythic thinker, either. He doesn't consider it paramount to relive the past epochs of the Israelite dramas. Okay, then, where does that leave him?

Meir would rather participate in a coming drama—to lead the charge in the next and final chapter of Jewish history. He sees himself as a team captain of the Jews. He will carry out his leadership roles on the field of battle and in the theater of confrontation, struggle and war. In the dramatic unfolding of time, as he sees the world, we are in the metaphoric fourth quarter and the clock is running down. Rabbi Meir is out there to lead the forces of the one God of the Jewish people as they celebrate their deserved victory when the time runs off the clock.

And Rabbi Meir fully expects his team, the Jews, to win the game, the ultimate Super Bowl. That victory will trigger not just a celebration but a new epoch. The team calls it the Age of the Messiah, that distant galaxy of wish and fantasy where kingdoms are restored and created.

Keep in mind, as you get to know him, that Rabbi Meir is a total fan—a fanatic—of his side. A celebrity himself, he roots for the other celebrities on his team. He identifies with them and, when they win, it lifts his spirits. The dual actions of rooting and competing in the contest are primary to this personality. The outcome of the game is important, but secondary to Rabbi Meir, because he has no doubt that victory is at hand.

Our God is Number One

I call Rabbi Meir, the next person you meet in the synagogue, a celebrity because that is his self-proclaimed status. Performing on the world's center stage, he lets us know that he is a star member of the cast of the Chosen People. He is a confident monotheist who has an exciting story. As he tells it, the gods now are engaged in a continual conflict and competition. And, then, at some point in the future, there will be a final match when idolatry will lose. The victory will go to the one true God over his false and worthless competitors.

Our celebrity-monotheist exhorts everyone in the synagogue simultaneously with both vivid and vague visions of a cosmic war in heaven and on Earth. Rabbi Meir tells us about the coming state of affairs for the Jewish people. Our destiny will be fulfilled at the end of time in a promised culmination.

All of this drama is simply stated in the first section of the Aleinu prayer (which we first cited above, in connection with the performer in the context of the Rosh Hashanah services):

> It is our duty to praise the Lord of all things,
> to ascribe greatness to him who formed the world in the beginning,
> since he has not made us like the nations of other lands,
> and has not placed us like other families of the earth,
> since he has not assigned unto us a portion as unto them,
> nor a lot as unto all their multitude.
>
> For we bend the knee and offer worship and thanks before the supreme King of kings, the Holy One, blessed be he,
> who stretched forth the heavens and laid the foundations of the earth,
> the seat of whose glory is in the heavens above,
> and the abode of whose might is in the loftiest heights.
>
> He is our God; there is none else: in truth he is our King; there is none besides him;
> as it is written in his Torah, "And you shall know this day, and lay it to your heart that the Lord he is God in heaven above and upon the earth beneath: there is none else."
> (Koren Siddur, p. 180)

Rabbi Meir cheers on, urging his values on others like that of a team coach or captain in a locker room before a crucial game. But, wait. There is another important vagary. This is not yet a real game. In his synagogue prayers, the celebrity-monotheist does not encourage and exhort his team of worshippers to go out and trample the identified competing teams. Rather, his call in his liturgy is figuratively to act out a competition—akin to participating in a fantasy religion league—to imagine that the ultimate showdown is nigh, to conjure a vision of the minutes ticking down at the close of the game. The end of time, the end to the struggle and the ultimate victory of the team of the one true God over the team of the false Gods is at hand. The conclusion of the Aleinu prayer finally and forcefully proclaims the details:

> We therefore hope in you, O Lord our God,
> that we may speedily behold the glory of your might,
> when you will remove the abominations from the earth,
> and the idols will be utterly cut off,
> when the world will be perfected under the kingdom of the Almighty,
> and all the children of flesh will call upon your name,
> when you will turn unto yourself all the wicked of the earth.
>
> Let all the inhabitants of the world perceive and know that unto you every knee must bow, every tongue must swear.
>
> Before you, O Lord our God, let them bow and fall;
> and unto thy glorious name let them give honor;
> let them all accept the yoke of your kingdom,
> and do you reign over them speedily, and forever and ever.
>
> For the kingdom is yours, and to all eternity you will reign in glory;
> as it is written in your Torah, "The Lord shall reign forever and ever."
>
> And it is said, "And the Lord shall be king over all the earth: in that day shall the Lord be One, and his name One."

Let me measure the dimensions of this archetype. Like those of the mystic and meditator, he is a powerful personality type without any specific proclivity of status or profession. I could have called this archetype a "triumphalist." That labeling bears a pejorative connotation when it is used by social scientists to describe a type of leader or his groups. So, rather than use that term, which is the best existing label, I chose to make up for him a new name without any baggage, that is, the celebrity-monotheist.

And, indeed, this is the most potentially controversial and even negative archetype of those ideal people whom you meet in the synagogue. He may turn out to be a forceful competitor with combative rhetoric. And there is the danger that his friends could hear his bellicose cheering and cross the line. They could potentially be cajoled into going beyond enthusiastically rooting for a hoped-for fantasy victory leading to a Messianic Age. They could be moved beyond argumentative rhetoric to take up antagonistic actions to bring about their hoped-for triumph.

Misdirected and misguided, religion in a triumphal mode can—and, sadly, often does—breed violence and terrorism.

In relation to the other archetypes of the synagogue, I associate this archetype in one respect with the priest, who is somewhat of a public and political personality. But the priests are entrenched in their world of present day discipline, their recollections of the Temple rites and all that attends to them—those notions that we spelled out in our previous chapter on the priest's prayers. They do not care much for the way that Rabbi Meir tries to turn the attention of the synagogue to a distant dream of salvation. They offer a viable set of saving graces through acts of worship, religious institutions and the worldview that surrounds those core values. When they do reluctantly buy into the celebrity's messianic message, it takes a recognizably priestly form. They accept a vision of the age of redemption that includes for them a complete package deal: the rebuilding of the city of Jerusalem and the Temple, and the restoration of the sacrificial service.

As I note, Rabbi Meir shares few values with Rav Aharon the scribe or with the ideal type of Deborah the meditator. Neither of these personalities particularly wants to divert the focus from his or her day-to-day religious habits, conceptions and values and turn instead to primarily await the messiah and the end of days. When those archetypes do accept elements of a vision of the transformation at the end of time, it takes a specific shape; they see it as an era of peace and not war, a tame time of tranquility when the predator will befriend the prey. The priest's vision of political and religious triumph, and the rebuilding of the Temple, takes a back seat to their notions that the redeemer will change the natural order of things and bestow a universal peace upon the land. Rather, it will be the perfect future age in which the scribe and meditator can practice their way of life based on the Torah— just as they do in the present—but, finally, in the new age, they can do all that without fears or disruptions.

In our ideal synagogue, the celebrity articulates his agenda of a dramatic public and political Messianic Age and the priests, scribes and meditators hear a different model. The celebrity's message of the end of days comes to wider expression in multiple layers of narrative. The other archetypes attach what they want onto the articulation of the universal recognition of our one God. They append onto the vision of the celebrity their expectations of the rebuilding of Jerusalem, the city and the Temple, of the change of the natural order and, also, of the mystical resurrection of the dead.

As I get know the celebrity Rabbi Meir better, I understand that his core formative principles coincide with the essence of a generic warrior archetype—a character who, in fact, is mainly absent as an attendee at the synagogue. As I said earlier, in the synagogue's incarnation, the combatant does not do any actual fighting. An imagined mythic conflict is conducted on his behalf by a god who will vanquish the enemy idols at the end of days. "Our God will be number one" is the signature cheer of the essential narrative of this archetype.

In sum, the celebrity-monotheist shows confidence and derives pride from his sense of being one of the chosen and in his certainty in ultimate triumph. He speaks boldly of the moment of his group's inevitable victory, couched as his faith in his God's ascendancy and superiority. And, as I showed above, the Aleinu serves as a pristine liturgical case in point for this archetype.

Not surprising, in speaking about that prayer in a roundabout way, some rabbinic interpreters tried to tell us this. They explained the prayer's origin in history instead of enlightening us more fully about how this prayer promises us a future conflict and conquest. The rabbis suggested that the victorious biblical warrior-prophet Joshua composed the

Aleinu in the distant past during one of his triumphs, either when he crossed the Jordan to enter the Promised Land or after his victory at the battle of Jericho. [See *Arugat ha-Bosem*, ed. by E. E. Urbach, 3 1962, 468–71.] The spectrum of time merges for the rabbis as they talk about their theory of the origins of the prayer so as to shed light on what this celebrity-monotheist's prayer tells us about his expectations for the future.

The stories referenced in the celebrity-monotheist's prayers—the hints and suggestions in the synagogue about the messianic redemption—are not only about confrontation, conflict and victory. There are alternatives in the prayers of the synagogue that touch on the messianic theme in a more peaceful manner, one more acceptable to the scribes and the meditators.

To help make this clear, I introduce you briefly to Beruryah—a hybrid variety of celebrity-monotheist combined with elements of other archetypes. While Beruryah is equally certain of the starring role of the Jews and of their God in the script of world history, she is more irenic, more peaceful in her visions of the future, of the final act of the drama.

In the Talmud, there are a few stories about a morally admirable woman named Beruryah, who was the wife of an ancient Rabbi Meir. She stands out as a rare woman-scholar in the male-dominated rabbinic culture. To give you a flavor for what the Talmudic Beruryah stood for, here is one of the traditions about her from the Babylonian Talmud, tractate Berakhot 10a:

> Certain brigands who were in the neighborhood of Rabbi Meir used to trouble him greatly. He prayed that they die. Beruryah his wife said to him, "Why do you pray this way?
>
> "Because it is written (in Psalms 104:35), 'Let sins cease...?' Is 'sinners' written? Rather 'sins' is written.
>
> "Furthermore, cast your eyes to the end of the verse, 'And they are wicked no more.' Since sins will cease, the sinners will be wicked no more.
>
> "So pray that they repent and be wicked no more."
>
> He prayed for them, and they repented.

Much like the Talmudic figure of that name, my imaginary character Beruryah encapsulates a moral superiority. In addition, we attribute to her some of the prophet Isaiah's anti-war visions of salvation at the end of days, which we judge to be a morally superior vision of the end-times. After some supernatural transformation of the nature of humankind, scripture reports in Isaiah chapter two, "...and they shall beat their swords into plowshares, and their spears into pruning hooks; nation shall not lift up sword against nation, neither shall they learn war anymore."

Although this model of the age of redemption is not spelled out unequivocally in the prayers, you do find echoes of such notions in several places, including the Kedushah for Shabbat in the Shaharit service, as follows:

> Reader — We will sanctify your name in the world even as they sanctify it in the highest heavens, as it is written by the hand of your prophet: And they called one unto the other and said,

> Cong. — Holy, holy, holy is the Lord of hosts: the whole earth is full of his glory.

> Reader — Then with a noise of great rushing, mighty and strong, they make their voices heard, and, upraising themselves toward the Seraphim, they exclaim over against them, Blessed.

> Cong. — Blessed be the glory of the Lord from his place.

> Reader — From your place shine forth, O our King, and reign over us, for we wait for thee. When wilt thou reign in Zion? Speedily, even in our days, do thou dwell there, and forever. May you be magnified and sanctified in the midst of Jerusalem your city throughout all generations and to all eternity. O let our eyes behold your kingdom, according to the word that was spoken in the songs of your might by David, your righteous anointed:

> Cong. — The Lord shall reign forever, your God, O Zion, unto all generations. Praise you the Lord.

> Reader — Unto all generations we will declare your greatness, and to all eternity we will proclaim your holiness, and your praise, O our God, shall not depart from our mouth

forever, for thou art a great and holy God and King. Blessed art thou, O Lord, the holy God.

The liturgy does not negate directly the triumphal celebrity monotheist's vision. What it does, however, is present a more morally balanced and less confrontational scenario by intermixing mystical concepts with messianic themes in formulating elements of the ultimate praise of God.

Another articulation in the synagogue of the celebrity's views is the special Kaddish that is recited in the funeral service at a cemetery. This is the Kaddish that is said by the mourning children after the burial of their parents. This prayer has no explicit irenic intent. Rather, it's an interesting amalgamation—an olio, if you will—of some messianic notions with the priestly images of Temple and Jerusalem, its city, along with the mystic's idea of the resurrection of the dead at the end of days:

> Mourners — May his great name be magnified and sanctified in the world that is to be created anew, where he will quicken the dead, and raise them up into life eternal; will rebuild the city of Jerusalem, and establish his temple in the midst thereof; and will uproot all alien worship from the earth and restore the worship of the true God. O may the Holy One, blessed be he, reign in his sovereignty and glory during your life and during your days, and during the life of all the house of Israel, even speedily and at a near time, and say ye, Amen.

> Cong. and Mourners — Let his great name be blessed forever and to all eternity.

I find yet another instance of a messianic medley of expressions of the celebrity-monotheist in a passage from the beginning of the central part of the Musaf, the Additional Service Amidah for Rosh Hashanah:

> Now, therefore, O Lord our God, impose your awe upon all your works, and your dread upon all that you have created, that all works may fear you and all creatures prostrate themselves before you, that they may all form a single band to do your will with a perfect heart, even as we know, O Lord our God, that dominion is yours, strength is in

your hand, and might in your right hand, and that your name is to be feared above all that you have created.

Give then glory, O Lord, unto your people, praise to them that fear you, hope to them that seek you, and free speech to them that wait for you, joy to your land, gladness to your city, a flourishing horn unto David your servant, and a clear shining light unto the son of Jesse, your anointed, speedily in our days.

Then shall the just also see and be glad, and the upright shall exult, and the pious triumphantly rejoice, while iniquity shall close her mouth, and all wickedness shall be wholly consumed like smoke, when you make the dominion of arrogance to pass away from the earth.

And you, O Lord, shall reign, you alone over all your works on Mount Zion, the dwelling place of your glory, and in Jerusalem, your holy city, as it is written in your Holy Words, The Lord shall reign forever, your God, O Zion, unto all generations. Praise be the Lord.

The prayer repeats the familiar themes and announces new sub-themes, namely that wickedness and arrogance will be banished at the end of days; gladness and a shining light will characterize the new era, an age that will be imposed with awe and dread.

The dour, even militant tenor of the last two examples, and the mainly peaceful tendency of the one that precedes it, show us that there are different flavors of the celebrity-monotheist visions.

These contrasts are more dramatically and bluntly juxtaposed in another illustration, in a ritual at the Seder meal. On Passover night, we hope and expect with joy that the prophet Elijah will visit the Seder at every Israelite house. And, so, we pour a cup of wine for the prophet, the herald of the coming of the end of days and of the transformation of conflict into peace.

During the Seder, right before the recitation of the psalms of the Hallel, when we open the door to greet Elijah, the precursor of the peaceful messiah, the instructions in the Haggadah prescribe, "The fourth cup is poured and the door is opened. Say the following":

Pour out your wrath upon the nations that do not acknowledge you, and upon the kingdoms that do not call upon your name. For they have devoured Jacob and laid waste his habitation. Pour out your indignation upon them, and let the wrath of your anger overtake them. Pursue them with anger, and destroy them from beneath the heavens of the Lord.

Here, then, outside of the synagogue, in the Seder recited at home, a sentiment about the coming age is stated most strongly. The liturgist calls on God to confront his foes, to vent his indignation, wrath and anger, and to destroy those who do not recognize our God.

Prayer-jacking and Martyrs

When you hijack a plane, you violently take control of the whole entity and fly it to the place you choose. When you hijack a liturgy, you try to do the same. The celebrity-monotheist tried to hijack the Unetanneh Tokef prayer, a liturgy of the scribe and mystic from the High Holy days that we discussed above. He tried to make it his own, by writing a story about its authorship and origin.

I've emphasized how I judge that, in all cases, prayer origins are secondary to their essences. Certainly, here, in the case of such a powerful poem, thinking about who was its ancient writer detracts from it and distracts us from the impact of the complex religious messages embedded in the prayer.

Rabbi Reuven Hammer summarized the strange authorship story of this liturgy. As we recall, it speaks dramatically about how God decides on Rosh Hashanah who shall live and who shall die. Hammer calls the origin account for this liturgy a "legend":

It is little wonder that this poem gave birth to legend. It is said that it was recited by Rabbi Amnon (Mainz, c. eleventh century), who had failed to reject a proposal of apostasy immediately and instead asked for three days to consider it. When he did not agree to give up his faith, he was taken away and tortured brutally. It was Rosh Hashanah, and he asked his disciples to take him to the synagogue, where he interrupted the service and recited this prayer in order to sanctify the name of God. Upon completing the recitation, he died. Later, the legend continues, he appeared to Rabbi Kalonymus in a dream and asked that this prayer be recited each year. Moving as this legend is, it should not distract us from the *piyyut* itself, the subject of which is not martyrdom, but human responsibility and the possibility for change, as we face the judgment of our creator.

Sadly, in real Jewish history, martyrdom did occur many times. However, imposing a gory martyrdom background origin-story on this particular liturgy is a violent means of taking us away from the inherent mystical and scribal images of the prayer and its potent meanings.

The celebrity's darker side comes to the forefront here. The description in the authorship legend is actually more graphic than what Rabbi Hammer recounts. In the full version of the legend, the Christian authorities dismembered the martyr and delivered him back to the synagogue without limbs. In his us-versus-them world, the celebrity archetype sometimes uses a gruesome means to stir his team's emotions against his imagined enemy.

In fact, while we are on the subject, there is a poignant martyr's prayer recited on Yom Kippur in the Musaf service. The prayer begins, "These I recall," in Hebrew, *Eilleh Ezkrah*. It's an old and venerable narrative account from the time of the Crusades in the Middle Ages. It tells us about the much earlier torture and killing of ten rabbis by the Romans in Israel after the Bar Kokhba revolt in 135 CE.

At his death at the hands of the Romans, with his last breath, Rabbi Akiva recited the Shema. The scribe-martyrs of Eilleh Ezkrah chose to recite the Shema with their last breaths, to perish with their declaration of the love of God, his Torah and their loyalty to his commandments.

The martyrdom account of Rabbi Akiva mournfully describes, "As they scraped his skin with iron combs, he recited the Shema, accepting the yoke of the sovereignty of heaven... His soul left him as he uttered the word 'One.'"

Other accounts of medieval martyrs have them reciting the Aleinu as their last utterances. In 1171, at Blois France during the Crusades, Barry Freundel (*Why we Pray What we Pray*, NY 2010, p. 228, citing Raphael Posner, et. al., ed., *Jewish Liturgy: Prayer and Synagogue Service through the Ages*, Jerusalem, 1975, p. 110) tells us the following:

> ...thirty-four Jewish men and seventeen Jewish women were burned at the stake because they refused to accept Baptism. The contemporaneous records of this act of martyrdom tell of these Jews singing Aleinu with a "soul-stirring" melody as they gave their lives to sanctify God's name.

These were celebrity-martyrs, who elected to die proclaiming the ultimate triumph of one God. No doubt, the victims at Blois loved Torah and commandments. And, for certain, the rabbis tortured to death who recited the Shema were confident in the ultimate victory of God and in the coming of the Messianic Age of redemption for the Jews and all humankind. But, when you choose your dying words, that comes from the essence of your identity. The core of your being rules the priorities of your choices. The creators of martyr accounts formulate matters simply. When a Jew faces martyrdom, he chooses as his last prayer that which embodies the essence of his personality. A rabbi-scribe in Roman times will recite the Shema. A resisting-celebrity in the Crusades will recite the Aleinu.

Are the accounts of martyrdom accurate to what happened? We cannot know more than what the later narrators elect to tell us about our ancient and medieval martyrs.

Sadly, we have had multitudes more tragedies in modern times. Official synagogue representation of the modern martyrs of the Holocaust, in text or ritual, has been rare. But, recently, American Conservative Judaism did choose to develop a Kaddish for death camps. Based, in part, on the last passages of Andre Schwarz-Bart's novel, *The Last of the Just* (New York, 1960), this ritual and text was originally incorporated into the Yom Kippur Martyrology of the 1972 *Mahzor for Rosh Hashanah and Yom Kippur* of the Rabbinical Assembly.

Rabbi Jules Harlow, editor of the *Mahzor,* described the impetus for the innovation as follows:

The text of the Martyrology incorporates rabbinic narratives about some of the martyred rabbis as well as words from the Psalms and from modern authors, including Bialik, Hillel Bavli, Nelly Sachs, A.M. Klein and Soma Morgenstern. At the conclusion of the narrative recalling martyrs of various times, we wanted to articulate the tension between faith on the one hand and, on the other, the questioning doubt which arises out of our confrontation with even the recollection of the murder of those Jews. And we did not want to articulate that tension in an essay or in a footnote . . .

We chose the statement of faith par excellence in Jewish tradition, the Mourner's Kaddish. After the death of a family member, when a Jew has perhaps the strongest reasons to question God, he or she is obliged to stand in public to utter words in praise of God.

Harlow explained to me the motives of the liturgy in a personal letter (March 2, 1989):

We interrupt these words, this statement of faith, with the names of places where Jews were slaughtered, places which therefore cause us to raise questions, to have doubts. The tension is resolved, liturgically, by the last four lines, whose words are uninterrupted by the names which give rise to questioning, thus concluding in a framework of faith.

Harlow added that there are intentionally seventeen places named, signifying that life, represented by the Hebrew *Chai*, numerically eighteen, "...can never be complete, can never be the same, after such slaughter." This is not noted in the prayer book.

In the new Kaddish, the original Aramaic text alternates with a register of sites of extermination in this compound liturgy:

> We rise
> *Yitgadal*
>   Auschwitz
> *ve'yitkadash*
>   Lodz
> *Sh'mei raba*
>   Ponar
> *b'alma di v'ra khir'utei,*
>   Babi Yar

v'yamlikh malkhutei
          Maidanek
b'hayeikhon u-v'yomeikhon
          Birkenau
u-v'hayei d'khol beit yisrael,
          Kovno
ba-agala u-vi-z'man kariv,
          Janowska
v'imru amen.

Y'hei sh'mei raba m'vorakh l'alam u-l'almei almaya.

Yitbarakh v'yishtabah
          Theresienstadt
v'yitpa'ar v'yitromam
          Buchenwald
v'yitnasei v'yit-hadar
          Treblinka
v'yit'aleh v'yit-halal
          Vilna
sh'mei d'kudsha,
          Bergen-Belsen
brikh hu l'ela
          Mauthausen
min kol birkhata v'shirata,
          Dachau
tushb'hata v'nehemata
          Minsk
da-amiran b'alma,
          Warsaw
v'imru amen.

Y'hei sh'lama raba min sh'maya v'hayim aleinu v'al kol yisrael,
          v'imru amen.
          Oseh shalom b-m'romav, hu ya'aseh shalom aleinu v'al kol yisrael,
          v'imru amen.

I cite here the Kaddish of the *Siddur Sim Shalom* (edited by Jules Harlow, 1985, pp. 841-843). The more extensive Kaddish of the Martyrology of the Day of Atonement is not limited to communities and camps where the Jews were killed during the Second World War. It includes Kishinev, Hebron, Mayence, Usha and Jerusalem, places where Jews were slaughtered in other historical eras.

The special Kaddish is an intermixed text with no narrative. It creates an intrusion into the set liturgy, thus wanting to depict the disruption of death within the static reality of the people. It is a violent representation. Names of locations of destruction, in language read from left to right, confront the doxology of praise, in the liturgy recited from right to left.

The new Kaddish confuses and traumatizes the soothing cadence of the expected traditional prayer. This unconventional form of the prayer breaks the somber beat of the chant of the Kaddish, one of the sure rhythms and universally recognized prayers of the synagogue.

It also mixes the main elements of a martyrology into a quintessential prayer of the mystic. Those tragic ideas and recollections are more comfortably situated in the prayers and personality of the celebrity.

Writing this prayer was a bold idea, a valiant try at getting recognition of the mythic meaning of the Holocaust into the standard service of the synagogue. But it failed, because it chose too freely to mix the notions of the celebrity archetype of prayer into the Kaddish, the doxology of the mystic. The current conservative Mahzor, *Lev Shalem*, published in 2010, omits the prayer from the service.

The celebrity-monotheist, as you easily can tell, is not my favorite among the archetypes I meet in the synagogue. He is, however, a legitimate, vocal and dramatically substantial member of our congregation. We *do* need to meet him, to know him, to respect the integrity of his messages and try to direct his powerful energies to positive spiritual and cultural goals.

The Kiddush

Kiddush *Hebrew*

— *n*

1. a special blessing said before a meal on Sabbaths and festivals, usually including the blessing for wine or bread
2. a reception usually for the congregants after a service at which drinks and snacks are served and grace is said
[from Hebrew *qiddūsh* sanctification]

—Collins English Dictionary, 2009

After the *davening* on *Shabbos*, my perfect *shul* has a Kiddush—a luncheon—in the social hall downstairs. It's a light collation for socializing. One big table is set up for the buffet of food and wine and others are arrayed for the congregants to sit and eat and talk. The tables are covered by clean white tablecloths.

My friends and I each get a glass of wine and some food, a bowl of hot synagogue cholent, slow-cooked stew of meat, potatoes and beans made especially for the Shabbat lunch. We wait to drink and eat until the leader offers the toast, though that is known in the *shul* not as the toast, but as the Kiddush-Prayer.

The Hebrew word *Kiddush*, used for both that communal synagogue lunch and for the prayer, means "sanctification," or making holy.

On the Sabbath day, the toast is quite brief. It consists for most who recite it of two biblical passages about the Sabbath, followed by an invitation and a blessing over the wine:

> And the Children of Israel shall observe the Shabbat, by establishing the Shabbat for their generations as an eternal covenant. Between Me and the Children of Israel it is an eternal sign, that in six days the Lord made the heavens and the earth, and on the seventh day he ceased from work and rested. (Exodus 31:16-17)

Remember the Shabbat day to sanctify it. Six days you shall labor and do all your work, but the seventh day is Shabbat for the Lord your God; you shall not do any work — you, your son and your daughter, your manservant and your maidservant, and your cattle, and the stranger who is in your gates. For in six days the Lord made the heavens, the earth, the sea, and all that is in them, and rested on the seventh day.

Therefore the Lord blessed the Shabbat day and made it holy. (Exodus 20:7-10)

Attention, distinguished ones, rabbis, guests and colleagues!

Blessed are you, Lord our God, King of the universe, who creates the fruit of the vine.

That's a simple enough toast—or, I should say, prayer. As a performer archetype, the leader recites the verses from the Torah script appropriate to the occasion. As a meditator archetype, he mindfully calls attention to the wine that is to be drunk and recites its blessing.

On Friday night, the Kiddush that is recited prior to the Sabbath meal is a slightly more complex toast. It starts out with Torah verses and the wine blessing. And then it gets more interesting:

There was evening, there was morning: The sixth day.

And the heavens and the earth and all that filled them were complete.

And on the seventh day God completed the labor he had performed, and he refrained on the seventh day from all the labor which he had performed. And God blessed the seventh day and he sanctified it, for he then refrained from all his labor—from the act of creation that God had performed. (Genesis 1:31, 2:1-3)

Attention, distinguished ones, rabbis, guests and colleagues!

Blessed are you, the Lord our God, King of the Universe, who creates the fruit of the vine.

Blessed are you, Lord our God, King of the Universe, Who sanctified us with his commandments, and hoped for us, and with love and intent invested us with his sacred Sabbath, as a memorial to the deed of Creation. It is the first amongst the holy festivals, commemorating the exodus from Egypt. For you chose us, and sanctified us, out of all nations, and with love and intent you invested us with your Holy Sabbath. Blessed are you, Sanctifier of the Sabbath.

The evening Kiddush is thus a short home liturgy that recalls the mythic beginnings of the world and of the Jewish nation. The archetypal tone of its last paragraph is that of the scribe (invoking the commandments, love and the Exodus) with a dash of celebrity-monotheist thrown in for good measure: "For you chose us ... out of all nations."

Table Talk

At the table on one ideal Sabbath, I sat together with my friends on folding chairs, with those people I met in the synagogue. After saying Amen to the Kiddush toast, we all took a sip of the wine. Rabbi Meir and Beruryah, the two ideal celebrity-monotheists, were not at all shy or reticent. They joined in an earnest discussion based loosely on some news story or event in Israel or Washington, D.C. of the past week. That repartee revealed a bit about how to read and reconcile the varieties of apparently dissimilar messianic expectations that are present in the synagogue services.

The discussion got lively as the others joined in. Our synagogue personalities debated whether they thought the celebrity-monotheist positions meshed or clashed with those of the other archetypes of the synagogue.

All things considered, this table talk did not shed that much light on any grand conceptions of the classical Jewish visions of the Messianic Age or reveal any splendid version of the theological underpinnings of Judaism.

The conversation that ensued among my archetype friends *did* try to account solely and somewhat humbly for a few diverse and complex goals and purposes of the services of the synagogue. Each archetype in turn put in plain words the crux of what the synagogue meant to them.

Here, in summary, are their ruminations at that Shabbat social chat, started off by Esther, an inquisitive non-archetypal congregant.

Congregant Esther: With all the world events of the past week, I wondered if the messiah will be coming soon. And I started to worry about the future of the Jewish people and of Judaism.

Rabbi Meir (the militant celebrity-monotheist): I believe the destiny of the Jews is clear. The new age will come soon and, in that time, all the nations of the earth will acknowledge the sovereignty of our God, and he will utterly destroy the idolatrous unbelievers. Every time I go forth from the synagogue into the street, I recite the Aleinu and recall this promise for the future.

Beruryah (the peaceful celebrity-monotheist): I agree in essence with Rabbi Meir and look forward to salvation and the new epoch. But, I hasten to add that, in my vision of the future, the new age will dawn with less violence and destruction. And I focus on the time further into the future, after the entire world has accepted the Lord and after God has transformed the essential nature of his creatures to be more loving and peaceful.

Rav Aharon (the scribe): I've got to admit that all this talk about the future makes me uncomfortable. If we shift our attention away from the present, then we may lose our focus on the need to keep the commandments, to obey the Torah, to love God today and seek his love in our lives *this* moment. The present obligations of the Jew are more urgent to me than the hope and expectation of some future conflict and salvation or some radical shift of nature. I can tolerate the idea that time will end for us all in redemption. But that cannot be my driving religious motivation. I admit, at times I think we say the Aleinu prayer too often. We conclude every service with an affirmation of a future redemption, when we really need more emphasis on the here and now of our Torah and its commandments.

Mr. Cohen (the priest): I have to share the concerns of Rav Aharon. We should not take our eyes too far off of the obligations that we have for religious meaning in the present. Yet we do agree with the future-directedness of Rabbi Meir, the celebrity. He has us in agreement with his monotheistic vision of the coming age because he specifically assures us that it will include a restoration for us of the Temple and the sacrificial rituals, a renewal of the tithes and heave-offerings, and that it will bring with it the rebuilding of the sanctuary and of the city of Jerusalem. We need to have those who join in the synagogue service recognize our agenda and values in the present and for the future age of redemption.

Deborah (the meditator): To me, the whole of the celebrity vision of future salvation is irrelevant. It is the specific, here in space and now in time, of every action each day, that I seek to imbue with layers of value and meaning. I want to focus in this moment on how to bestow my compassion, and ask God to bestow his, on all of his creatures. We should not use the synagogue to divert us to contemplate some indeterminate cosmic conflict. Those who wish to ponder such speculations should do so elsewhere, in some other Jewish context or, better yet, drop the matter entirely.

Hannah (the mystic): In my mystical quest, yes, I do seek ascent and transcendence. Hence, I cannot reject the notion of seeking from God a new and better place or time. In my reveries, I mix together the visions of the heavens with the images of the epochal end of days. At times, I come up with mystical, messianic ideas and personalities. It may not be neat and well packaged, but the celebrity's vision of the order of the end of days brings many of my ideas into play, especially my notion that the dead, whose souls continued on to heaven, once more shall be restored to earthly life. I endorse the centrality of these notions in the synagogue and accept it as a venue for both mystical and messianic contemplations.

Rabbi Meir: The messiah will come. He will bring with him the Messianic Age and we need to keep that belief, that narrative and that hope alive and vibrant and expectant in our lives. If not in the synagogue, then where will we contemplate such visions of hope?

Congregant Esther: Yes, but the future is not here and the messiah is not present in our synagogues. Your ideas and the stories that you tell sometimes seem incomplete and inconsistent. That confuses me. I'm hearing that turning to the celebrity's messianic future diverts us away from the synagogue.

Performer: From my vantage, the celebrity's visions serve our purposes in spades. The synagogue services are remarkable concerts, programs of a variety of exceptional artistic performances. The celebrity's conflicts punctuate our diverse performance programs with special dramas. In the course of our presentations, we move back and forth among the set pieces. We admit that a concert with pieces of significantly diverse styles—for example, in the world of music of having rock, rap, classical and baroque styles on the same program—may be too jarring to a listener, and that diversity may make it difficult to promote such an event. But, on the other hand, it makes for an intriguing show. Our synagogue service is that diverse and illustrious festival, which we inherited and which we need to live with, to continually refine and revive.

I n my role as the endless *davener,* and in my quest for the perfect prayer, I stand back and, yes, I agree in degrees with them all. Our Siddur is that wonderful complex and overlapping compilation of the expressions of prayers of those ideal people with whom I both assent and argue. And, finally, through that constant and endless practice and process of articulation and debate, I seek to find my God and to get to know better his favorite prayers.

Recike

The conversation among the archetypes of the synagogue continues on and on, week after week. To nourish that, I recommend that you consider my favorite recipe for the food for the Jewish soul.

Synagogue Cholent

Ingredients

One cup of scribal beans
One cup of priestly flour
One half-pint of meditator sauce
One tablespoon of celebrity powder
One pinch of mystical spices
One half cup of performer topping

Directions

Mix together the scribal beans and the priestly flour.
Fold in the meditator sauce and add the celebrity powder.
Sprinkle on the mystical spices.
Simmer for 3000 years.
Remove from the oven and coat liberally with performer topping.
Serve warm.
Will continually delight and perplex your company with its rich and varied textures and vibrant flavors.

Serves: One

The Shofar

Hollywood directors say it's hard to know how to end a film. I discovered for myself that it also can be hard to know how to conclude an account of a spiritual odyssey. Rather than to finish with a dialectic of discord or an abstract hope of unity, I feel it apt to finish with an insight into an actual dramatic synagogue conclusion. I opt to close now with some words about the final *shofar* blast at the close of the Yom Kippur fast, where the six disparate synagogue voices coalesce in brief shared characteristic prayers.

So let me recall for you one moment of recurring spiritual grandeur each year—the *shofar* blowing at the end of Yom Kippur in my unorthodox imagined synagogue.

I stand at the *bimah* with my friends. We are cleansed of our food and drink, and of our sins. After a day of prayer filled with compassion, we have let go of those negative habits, ideas and actions that separated us from one another. We see each other for who we are, separate personalities with diverse values and goals, united under a roof, in a community, sharing a past and future, and alive together in a productive, vibrant and respectful present.

The performer holds the *shofar* as the sun has dipped low in the west. He is ready to blow one great victorious blast, not to symbolize a triumph over external foes but to herald the start of a new year of greater optimism, free of the baggage that held us back, that kept us from seeing each other for who we are and that stopped us from respecting the integrity of that individualism.

The mystic begins to chant the Kaddish, not plaintively but, now, with the quick and upbeat tempo of the holiday season. He stops between each stanza, adding happy *ay-ay-ays*. He imagines the joy of the chant of the angels as they see the face of God, looking pleased that his worshippers are renewed and united with clean slates. They will try again this year, simply to do it all better. And, then, the performer stops toward the end of the prayer and turns to the scribe.

One time, the scribe sings out the Shema. Together, all join him with great clarity: Our God is one. Love god, love his Torah, perform his commandments. He turns back to his friend, the mystic.

Three times the mystic recites aloud with her friends the utterance that the angels sing before God, "Praised be the one whose glorious sovereignty is forever and ever."

Her fellow *davener*, the celebrity continues. "God is the God," the monotheist intones with the conviction, certainty and the daily persistence to face the world of adversity, to rise out of any setback, to transform suffering into sanctity, to perfect humanity, to bring a better age. Seven times, he repeats it for the seven days, for the constant vigilance that he must have. And, rising in intensity, they proclaim together, "God is the God."

The performer lifts the *shofar* and blows—not one-hundred times as they did in the services on Rosh Hashanah. Here, just one long blast will suffice. *Tekiah Gedolah*. This time, it is not an alarm to wake us as on Rosh Hashanah. It is an Amen, to send us forward to the new year together with loving-kindness as friends.

The friends join hands with the priest and begin to dance in a circle, singing, "*Leshanah haba*—this coming year in Jerusalem." May we be together in our new Jerusalem, a temple of shared worship, of service to ourselves and to each other and to God. *Baruch shehecheyanu*—blessed be God who has brought us to this time. The meditator recites this blessing to herself. We are alive, God has given us the gift to see ourselves mindfully in this moment, not in the past or the future. She looks from friend to friend and sees that they, too, paused to be in this moment, to celebrate together with thanks and compassion.

Sources

Listed in order of citation in this book.

Ismar Elbogen, *Jewish Liturgy*, Philadelphia, 1993.
Jeff Idelson, Baseball Hall of Fame, Cooperstown, New York.
Zev Chafetz, "The Right Way to Pray?" *The New York Times Magazine*, New York, Sept. 16, 2009.
James Kugel, *Prayers that Cite Scripture*, Cambridge, 2006.
Alan Mintz, *Hurban: Responses to Catastrophe in Hebrew Literature*, New York, 1984.
Rabbi E. Bar Shaul, *Mitzvah Valev*, Tel Aviv, 1956.
Encyclopedia of Synagogue Archetypes. a hypothetical book.
Michael F. Hammer, et. al., "Extended Y chromosome haplotypes resolve multiple and unique lineages of the Jewish priesthood," *Human Genetics*, 2009.
Yehuda Bauer, *Rethinking the Holocaust*, New Haven, 2000.
_____, *The Death of the Shtetl*, New Haven, 2010.
Mark Zbrowski and Elizabeth Herzog, *Life is with People*, New York, 1952.
Fiddler on the Roof, a 1964 musical play based on the work of Sholem Aleichem.
The New York Times, Herald Tribune, Journal American
Jon Kabat-Zinn, *Wherever You Go, There You Are: Mindfulness Meditation in Everyday Life*, New York, 1994.
E. E. Urbach, *Arugat ha-Bosem le-R. Abraham b. Azriel*, Jerusalem, 1962.
Reuven Hammer, *Entering Jewish Prayer: A Guide to Personal Devotion and the Worship Service*, New York, 1995.
Barry Freundel, *Why we Pray What we Pray*, New York, 2010.
Andre Schwarz-Bart, *The Last of the Just*, New York, 1960.

Prayer Books
The Koren Sacks Siddur, Jerusalem, 2009; referred to throughout this book as "Koren Siddur."
Siddur Sim Shalom for Shabbat and Festivals, New York, 1998.
Mahzor for Rosh Hashanah and Yom Kippur, New York, 1972.
Siddur Sim Shalom, ed. Jules Harlow, New York, 1985.
Mahzor Lev Shalem, New York, 2010.

Film
Bruce Brown, the film *Endless Summer*, 1966.

About the Author

Rabbi Tzvee Zahavy, Ph.D., was born and raised in New York City. He is an internationally recognized creative and imaginative expert in the fields of Judaism, Talmud and Jewish liturgy.

Dr. Zahavy received his BA in mathematics, master's degree in Jewish History, and rabbinic ordination from Yeshiva University, where he studied for four years with Rabbi Joseph B. Soloveitchik.

After receiving his Ph.D. in Religious Studies from Brown University, Dr. Zahavy was on the faculty of the University of Minnesota for nineteen years. He was promoted to full professor and was chairman of his department and director of the Center for Jewish Studies. He taught courses in Judaism, Jewish history and culture, Bible, World Religions, and seminars in classical Hebrew texts.

Dr. Zahavy received the Distinguished Teaching Award from the College of Liberal Arts, University of Minnesota. He has received numerous other grants and awards. He was a visiting professor at the University of California at Berkeley and at the College of William and Mary.

Dr. Zahavy has taught liturgy as an adjunct professor at the Jewish Theological Seminary of America in New York City.

His nine published books include these titles:

- *The Traditions of Eleazar Ben Azariah*, Brown Judaic Studies
- *The Mishnaic Law of Blessings and Prayers: Tractate Berakhot*, Brown Judaic Studies
- *The Talmud of the Land of Israel: Tractate Berakhot*, University of Chicago Press
- *Studies in Jewish Prayer*, University Press of America
- *The Talmud of Babylonia: An American Translation: Tractate Hullin*, 3 volumes, Brown Judaic Studies

Since 2006, his popular Judaica-oriented current-events blog, *Tzvee's Talmudic Blog* (Tzvee.blogspot.com), has logged more than one million page views. Dr. Zahavy is also active on Twitter, Facebook and LinkedIn.

Dr. Zahavy's Jewish Studies web site address is:
http://www.tzvee.com.

Reviews

"God's favorite prayers have all been right in plain sight for centuries, though never before experienced like this. With his characteristic blend of chutzpah and humor, Professor Rav Zahavy makes finding spiritual experiences into a real page turner! A fun, fascinating and totally refreshing way to finally learn how to pray."

—Dr. Arlene Rossen Cardozo, author of *Sequencing*, *Woman at Home* and *Jewish Family Celebrations*

"Tzvee Zahavy's artful melding of memoir, analysis, and typology enriches our understanding of liturgical experience and encourages us to emulate him by reflecting more thoughtfully on our own prayer lives."

—Rabbi Eliezer Diamond Ph.D., Associate Professor of Talmud and Rabbinics, Jewish Theological Seminary

"... An engaging, humanly sensitive introduction to the types of religious personalities whose views are expressed in the diverse parts of the Siddur and, more generally, in components of Jewish liturgical practices... A fine text for helping students and interested lay people gain an understanding and appreciation of the spiritual viewpoints expressed in Jewish liturgical texts."

—Joel Gereboff, Professor of Religious Studies, Arizona State University

"It is not often that one has the opportunity to share the authentic personal experiences of a distinguished scholar in the field of liturgy, who is also an award-winning teacher. These two elements stand out in Tzvee Zahavy's *God's Favorite Prayers*. Zahavy takes us on an amazing journey into the world of Jewish Prayer and into the personalities that make up the 'quorum' in the synagogue. His observations and insights will inspire people of all faiths, who truly seek out a way to make prayer, both personal and communal, a meaningful part of their lives."

—Rabbi Shimon Altshul, Director, the Ludwig and Erica Jesselson Institute for Advanced Torah Studies, Bar Ilan University

This book's Internet address is
http://www.godsfavoriteprayers.com.

8905502R0

Made in the USA
Charleston, SC
27 July 2011